Out of the Cocoon

A Young Woman's Courageous Flight from
the Grip of a Religious Cult

by
Brenda Lee

Robert D. Reed Publishers • Bandon, OR

Copyright © 2006 by Brenda Lee

All rights reserved.

This book is not affiliated with, approved or endorsed by the Watchtower Bible and Tract Society of New York, Inc., or any of its affiliates, divisions, corporations, or entities, or by Jehovah's Witnesses in any country or region.

Robert D. Reed Publishers
P.O. Box 1992
Bandon, OR 97411
Phone: 541-347-9882 • Fax: -9883
E-mail: 4bobreed@msn.com
web site: www.rdrpublishers.com

Typesetter: **Barbara Kruger**
Cover Designer: **Grant Prescott**

ISBN 1-931741-65-4

Library of Congress Control Number 2005931700

Manufactured, typeset and printed in the United States of America

Dedication

This book is dedicated to my son, **Derek**, my inspiration. Derek, you taught me what "living" and "loving" means. Stay physically and emotionally healthy and true to yourself. It's a joy to watch you grow into such an incredible young man. I adore and cherish you. And my love will *always* be there for you—unconditionally.

Acknowledgments

Jim S., you were the catalyst for this book. You once told me: "You never know where life will take you." Then you offered your hand and took me to some amazing places. Even though we couldn't take this journey together, thank you for showing me the way. I will never forget you.

My precious **Aunt B,** when I think of grandmother's kindness, I'll always think of you. Her joyful essence transcended more than one generation. Thank you for helping me alter the course of my life and for being the sunshine as I emerged from my cocoon.

Darlene, Donna, Felicia, Kerrie and Teri, you are such great friends. Thank you for graciously lending me your ears when I had ideas and for bravely voicing your opinions. You love me for who I am, and I am grateful to have you in my life. People don't need a lot of friends, just real ones—like you.

Dad-i-o, you taught me so much growing up, more than you might ever know. You are a wonderful father, and I love you. Do not blame yourself for the dissention in our family. I understand that you were doing the best you could. I hope someday you too can find the peace and happiness in your life that I have found in mine. Acceptance is liberating.

Mother, you will probably never read this book, but I want to thank you for all the sacrifices you made raising me. I regret that neither one of us is willing to change the path we have chosen for our lives, but I do wish you the best life has to offer. I understand your strong convictions because we were, after all, cut from the same cloth.

Stuart, thank you for lending me your editing expertise and for being so encouraging.

Contents

God grant me the serenity to accept the people I cannot change, the courage to change the one I can, and the wisdom to know it's me.
Author Unknown

Preface

Everyone has a story to tell, but few people are willing to share their private lives with the rest of the world. It's difficult to expose your past and dissect it under a microscope, knowing how terribly the truth can hurt—not only yourself but also those you love. Nevertheless, sometimes a story must be told.

Although this is a personal account about losing my childhood to a religious cult, searching for acceptance, and eventually triumphing over adversity, I believe it will mirror parts of your life as well, steadily drawing you in. Your own fears, strengths and dreams will be revealed, perhaps in ways you never imagined.

Let's face it. We all have emotional baggage. Every time we open the door to a new chapter in our lives or make a decision, this baggage tumbles out like an old tennis racket and influences our choices.

Perhaps you have never forgiven the father who abused you. Meanwhile, the rage and shame slowly fester inside. You may have encased yourself inside an emotional fortress because you don't feel you can trust others. Or maybe you have fallen into a lifestyle riddled with self-destructive addictions in an attempt to fulfill some ridiculous belief instilled during your childhood—one that still taunts you: "*You* are not good enough!" Possibly you have become bitter and cynical and have become snared by the victim trap. As a result, you may unconsciously push away those who would love you the way you need to be loved and nurtured.

Have you ever wondered why one person can take a monumental obstacle in stride, such as cancer, while another completely self-destructs over something as insignificant as waiting in line at a store? We all have decisions to make when we encounter adversity in our lives: "How will I handle this?" Circumstances don't control us. Our attitude does.

I learned at the tender age of nine that while I could not readily change the hostile world I saw around me, I could change the world *within* me. Like a pupa, I embraced my metamorphosis. When I felt alone, depressed, and even desperate, I took pen in hand and opened my heart. Writing wasn't just therapy, it was my savior.

I believe the difference between a person's choosing life over death, loving over hating and nurturing over destroying depends on two things: hopes and dreams. Hopes and dreams are the catalysts for positive thinking and the anchors for human survival. There is a passage I read twenty years ago. The poignant message simply admonished: "Never take away someone's hopes and dreams, for it may be all he/she has left." You will find these words bolded throughout my story as a reminder of how frequently I clung to those words.

As you relive my story, I will take you through the darker recesses of my life to emerge with me *Out of the Cocoon*. Through this transformation, I have acquired a certain degree of redemption and peace. I have found the courage to face my demons, my past.

If you look into the depths of your past—into your very heart and soul—I'm certain you will unearth the treasures in you that are just waiting to be discovered. Whatever you do, don't be afraid to lay claim to what you deserve and take flight. *You* are worth it.

Chapter 1: All Alone in the World

APRIL 1, 1974:

Long ago it began...the life of a child too young to know the torment and torture she would experience in her years to come—the agony of life. Seclusion, weariness and loneliness from within herself she would know. Why this agony? Maybe it was her parents, or maybe it was herself, but mostly it was her environment, a world in which she could not cope with life and the people in her life. As she viewed the grotesque, blood-spattered bodies that lay before her, she reflected on her past with anxiety.

Jaime's childhood was normal. She ran, played and laughed with the other children. But then it happened. At the age of ten, her life drastically changed. But even more drastic was the change she saw in her parents and friends. Jaime knew she could no longer have fun. She had no idea what was happening.

Jaime entered a school that she hated. It seemed to be a downfall. But there she found friends. True friends that she would enjoy life with—until the day her parents said "No more." It seemed her parents didn't trust her. But why? She gave them no reason to. They seemed so overprotective and selfish. It seemed they wanted to keep her all to themselves.

Was she to become a hermit? What is life without friends? These questions kept crossing her mind.

Jaime was so afraid she'd go mad. She thought, "There must be a way out." Out of this world? Yes, there were drugs, but they were only temporary. She would have to find a permanent way to solve her problem. She thought about this day and night. Then the thought hit her—suicide? No, there must be a better way! Jaime tried talking the problem out with her parents, but all they did was confuse her. Even Jaime's friends seemed indifferent by now. No one seemed to care about what she thought.

When Jaime went home that night, her emotions were anger, despair and confusion. Jaime took the key to the gun cabinet. Slowly taking out the revolver, she stared at it as if in a trance. Would she shoot herself? She sat on the couch, stroking the gun and thinking about her problems. She just wanted to be free to live a normal childhood. Jaime finally decided she'd get rid of the problem by getting rid of the people that caused her problem.

The door to the hallway opened. Silently she took a butcher knife off the countertop. She made her way into the basement with the two weapons. Aiming precisely right, she pulled the trigger of the gun. Flesh ripped as the bullet penetrated her father's skull. He slumped over amid the hysterical screams of her mother. As Jaime's mother made her way towards her, Jaime pulled the knife out of her pocket and plunged it deep into her mother's stomach and heart. Now, Jaime would be free. But would she? The police would be after her. Panic gripped her soul. She heard a knock, just then, on the door upstairs. "This is the police; open up!" cried the haunting voices. She began shaking violently and as if possessed, the rage left her. She screamed a shrilling, piercing cry as the officers appeared on the steps.

Suddenly, she was awakened by her mother quietly saying, "It's OK now. You had a nightmare. Get up and get dressed for school. It wasn't real." But wasn't it? The anger returned and seemed to possess her again.

As you may have already guessed, "Jaime" was my alias. I was twelve years old when I wrote the above (unedited) short story. I rationalized that I should use a gun to shoot my dad because it would be a more merciful death. I really didn't want to kill my dad—I adored him—but I felt if I didn't, he would suffer immensely. In my inexperienced preteen mind, I wondered: "How can I leave him alive, knowing his child is in prison and his wife is dead?" A knife, however, was the weapon of choice for my mother—she deserved to feel the pain she had bestowed upon *me* as she slowly bled to death.

My teacher gave me an "A" on this story, but I wasn't hoping for a good grade. I was actually crying out for help, hoping some adult, somewhere, would recognize my pain and make it stop. I never intended to go through with this horrific fantasy because I realized ultimately I'd be hurting myself more.

What could make me so angry that I'd fantasize about taking away the lives of the very people who gave me life? To understand my fragile emotional state, we have to go back to the beginning when childhood innocence reigned and unconditional love was abundant—when I didn't feel all alone in the world.

Chapter 2: Growing a Farmer's Daughter

There is a garden in every childhood, an enchanted place where colors are brighter, the air softer, and the morning more fragrant than ever again.

Elizabeth Lawrence

In March of 1962, my mother felt contractions and less than one hour later I burst into this world with a fiery gusto. I relished hearing time and again how she barely made it to the hospital. As she sat in the admissions chair answering multiple questions—"Your name, ma'am?" "How do you spell that?" "Your address, ma'am?" "When did you feel the first contraction?" "Do you have insurance?"—she recalls impatiently admonishing the nurse, "I'm going to have this baby right here and now! Stop asking me such silly questions!"

A few days later, my parents brought me home to a rural farming community in Pennsylvania during a blinding blizzard. The snow was nearly three feet deep, not a typical winter for the Keystone State. My dad shoveled a path from the narrow, unplowed dirt road to the cellar so mom could carry me into our house.

My brother and sister had dark hair and dark complexions like my father, whereas, I had my mother's bright red hair, blue eyes and pale white skin, which turned beet red when I cried. And boy could I cry! The only child who developed colic, I howled an unrelenting wail that drove my mother and father to the brink of psychosis as they struggled to quiet me during my first three months of life. My father likes to recount how he lost his patience and swatted me on the bottom one night, which, of course, only induced louder screams. Every time he relives the story, I can sense his guilt. Perhaps my parents wondered, as they paced the bedroom floor in the middle of the night, me thrashing and wailing, why on Earth they hadn't spotted that unforgiving microscopic hole in my mother's diaphragm the night I was conceived.

Our homestead was full of history. The 150-year-old, three-story farmhouse with its large cement porch was situated on a hill surrounded by eighty acres of pine, oak, and maple trees. On the opposite side of the road stood a barely erect, massive two-story barn, streaked here and there with a faded red paint job from years gone by and weather-beaten, cracked windows laced with cobwebs.

This photograph was taken in 1982, years after the old homestead received a dramatic makeover.

No other homes were visible. Even the local gas station was miles away. At least the dirt road in front of our home provided some form of entertainment. When a car occasionally drove by, we were unavoidably drawn to the window—like bugs to a porch light—to see if it was someone we knew.

My father was born in our house and his grandmother had lived in it during the late 1800s. When he purchased it, however, it was dilapidated. Snakes called it home. There was no heat, no running water. But it was a mansion compared to the teeny three-room shack and "fragrant" outhouse that they had become accustomed to during their first four years of marriage. Despite its obvious need for renovation, the architecture was impressive: unusually wide wooden baseboards; archways crowning doorways; oval beveled glass in the doors and two or three brick fireplaces scattered throughout.

Father eventually added an indoor bathroom, installed a new roof, remodeled the kitchen and purchased modern appliances. He laid concrete in the cellar to replace the dirt floor and hung shingles on the exterior to eliminate the cold drafts blowing through the bare wood. In due time, the barn was filled with the typical farm equipment—a tractor, a wagon, a plow—and of course, inhabited by cows, pigs and thousands of mice.

I could see how hard my father worked to make us a real home and how much pride he had, even though we had so little in the way of material possessions. He spent every last dollar he earned as a mechanic on the railroad striving to put food on the table for a wife and three young children.

My most vivid memory of my father is watching him "putter around" outside until sunset (after putting in a full day at work), only to fall asleep well before bedtime in his recliner. His subsequent snoring rattled the chair similar to an earthquake, one quite capable of bumping the needle off the Richter scale. My fond memories of his strong work ethic stayed with me later in life as I began to emerge from my protective childhood cocoon.

Growing up on a farm had its good and bad points. Mowing acres of grass, weeding several gardens and throwing 40-pound bales of hay onto an aging wooden wagon kept me in good shape, out of trouble and always covered in scratches and Band-Aids™. Although I became quite the tomboy to survive farm life, I actually hated spending hours in the brutal summer sun tending our gardens and picking raspberries—quart after quart ad infinitum. If sunblock existed in those days, I didn't know about it, so I usually went to bed blistered. One night my back was so badly sunburned that I soaked my nightgown and bed sheets in water to ease the painful burning and itching. Little did I know it at the time but my homeopathic instincts were right on. The cool water seemed to surpass any other first aid I administered. Even still, sleep evaded me. I tossed and turned for three nights.

Despite all the drudgery of farm life, my reward always came later in the day when I devoured the sweet corn, fragrant vine-ripened tomatoes and succulent raspberries. My favorite recipe called for mashing raspberries in milk and sugar until the milk turned violet. My dad scoffed at me, "Brenda, you're ruining it!" I never understood why. It was absolutely delicious! Besides, drinking *lavender* milk made this humble farm girl feel incredibly chic.

Because my sister and brother were so much older (seven and ten years, respectively), I basically grew up as an only child. On rare occasions I was allowed to hang out with them, but this was definitely the exception rather than the rule. Instead, the customary interaction my brother had with me looked something like this: He'd pin me down and like a master puppeteer forcibly coerce my hands into slapping me repeatedly in the face while taunting, "Quit hitting yourself, dummy!" My brother was a colorful character whom I loathed. Even today I struggle to respect him. Later in this book, you'll learn why.

Since my sister and brother were undesirable as playmates, I enthusiastically shared the first eight years of my life with my cousins. The two boys were Evan (or "Punchy" as we liked to refer to him) and Tom. Punchy got his nickname because he liked to, well, *punch* people. Punchy liked to eat live locusts and pee on my bike, too. Punchy was definitely into deplorable behavior!

My female cousin, Deanna, was my best friend during those early years. Deanna had a little sister who always tried to tag along with us (*tried* being the operative word here). I could relate to her predicament. My siblings always did the same thing: excluding me when their friends visited. As a result, I thought it was only fitting that Deanna and I follow suit. At the first sign of her little sister, my favorite cousin and I sprinted away as quickly as we could and hid amongst some bushes or around a small storage shed. Once we successfully lost her pesky sibling, we'd giggle with glee, that is, until she found us again. [1]

I loved to tease my cousins. One of our favorite pastimes was playing Hide-and-Go-Seek inside my house. There were so many crevices and storage areas in our large farmhouse in which to squeeze a child's tiny body. But while everyone searched feverishly for me *inside* my house, I'd climb out my bedroom window (on the second floor), lower myself onto the roof below, and then cannonball to the grassy knoll below. Secretly concealing myself *outside*, I waited for them to scream, "Brenda, we give up!" I'd then sneak back into the house and sit calmly on the sofa. When they found me, I'd snidely inquire, "Why didn't you see me? I was right here the whole time!"

When I wasn't playing the queen of deception, my favorite hiding spot inside the house was an antique dresser with a small enclosure on top. Like a contortionist, I'd squeeze myself into its undersized confines, close the door, and wait for what felt like an eternity. I was delighted to sit in the dark pretzel-like and motionless while I anticipated the rustling in the room and giggles, followed by heavy sighs, and eventually the squeaking of the old wooden door as my cousins exited the room in humble defeat. I kept that hiding spot a secret for a long, long time.

Another favorite activity was to climb the twenty-foot ladder to the rafters in our barn and plummet into the soft hay below. After we dove in, the hay swallowed us whole,

---

[1] Children can be so cruel, but now that I am older, I see that children are like mirrors, reflections of those around them during those impressionable years. If you want to know what people in a child's life look like to him or her, watch the child's behavior and you will find out.

whilst the musty fragrance and hayseed permeated the air as we struggled to "swim" to the surface. Laughing so hard and barely able to stand, we sprinted like Olympic runners to the ladder to do it again and again. Looking back at it now, it's a miracle we didn't break our necks!

When we felt the need to be creative, we dug clay out of the ice-cold stream's muddy embankment and made lopsided pottery from it. My dad's barbecue pit in the side yard served as our kiln where we "fired" our creations.

If the forest beckoned us, we'd find adventure by exploring abandoned houses or swinging from vines. We loved climbing trees and hanging upside down until the blood rushed into our heads and made us stagger like eighty-pound drunken fools.

Our property was densely populated with fruit trees, so if our stomachs growled we devoured apples, pears, plums, cherries, walnuts, or whatever appealed to us. On good days I brought back flowers for my mom. On bad days, I brought back poison ivy.

If my cousins weren't available to play, I could usually coerce my brother into playing yard darts with me. These were eight-inch metal darts that you tossed across the yard and into a ring. (Manufacturers called *that* a toy!) Or I might entertain myself by repeatedly sliding down our porch stairs' green tubular railing. Wasps liked to build nests in the opening, however, so I had to be pretty quick when I got to the bottom to avoid getting stung in the derriere.

If I were in the mood to be daring, I'd utilize the four-inch ledge around our porch's perimeter as a balance beam. The clumsy gymnast lurking within tiptoed perilously on this outcrop, about fifteen feet off the ground. Ah, to live dangerously! Of course, I was only four-feet tall so the ground looked miles away.

Culture was introduced to me in the form of an antique piano, long forgotten in our cellar. Covered by a thick layer of dust and smelling rather musty, it reminded me of the dirty, wet bath towels mom hung from the clothesline nearby. Although my mom and dad were too poor to afford the music lessons that I begged them to provide, I'd frequently spend hours teaching myself songs from the accompanying songbook, battered and torn from years of use.

If I got lucky, my dad would take me for a ride on his tractor just for the fun of it. If he were especially jovial, he would let me sit on his lap and steer, and I'd be delighted as the coils under the holey steel seat bounced us up and down in wild abandon.

Most children dream of having lots of animals to care for, and I was no exception. I remember helping my father wrestle swine to the muddy ground so that he could give them a shot when they were sick. I was usually covered with more mud and feces than the pig but I loved the challenge of cornering a squealing pig!

Of course, no farm would be complete without cows. I remember on more than one occasion being chased up a tree by a bull and waiting for what felt like an eternity for it to go away. Once the massive beast wandered far enough away, I rushed to the electric fence that surrounded the pasture and, with a performance worthy of a professional limbo dancer, slid under it somewhat unscathed before the two-horned devil charged after me. More than once, however, the barbs from the fence ensnared my clothing, shocking and cutting me as I tried to free myself. If you have ever been introduced to an electric fence, you know how uncomfortable the experience can be. The electricity seems to shoot straight into your vital organs and afterwards you wonder how you kept from peeing your pants.

Cows, although adorable, are well known for their "meadow muffins." I recall many times running through the grassy pasture only to step in their soft, foul dung. It's distressing enough to do this when you have shoes on, but it's a truly indescribable experience when barefooted. If I were fortunate, I'd encounter a dried-up pie that had been baking in the sun for days and the damage was minimal. But as fate would usually have it, I gravitated to the fresh ones, which would instantly squish between my toes. (By the way, the stench takes days to wash off, so don't try this at home.) What followed was a very comical sight—a "fuming" (pungent and angry) child hopping on one foot up twelve stairs through the house and towards the bathroom, being very careful not to desecrate her mother's clean floors in the process.

Although the adult cows were menacing, I treasured the baby calves. I gave them unusual names, such as Spockiraustin—a combination of several characters in a popular TV series: Mr. Spock and Captain Kirk from *Star Trek* and Steve Austin from *The Six Million Dollar Man*. The quirky names I came up with always made my dad chuckle. At night I fed the babies milk, feeling a bond similar to the one a mother does after she nurses her baby. The calves cried vigorously when the milk was gone, and I cried silently when my dad took them off to be slaughtered. While I understood the need for our family to have food, it seemed like a contradiction in my mind to lavish love and care on animals and then turn them into hamburger and steaks. When the bloody meat came back from the butcher for us to wrap into neat little packages for the freezer, it sickened me to touch it. I was handling what was once my beloved pet. It felt no different than dicing up my dog. My father poked fun at me for being so squeamish; I don't think he understood the connection I had with the animals nor how deeply this affected me emotionally.

I absolutely adored my cat, Mac, a light-gray sweetie. Like a limp, rag doll in my arms, he exhibited boundless affection and love. He was my baby. But one day, I caught my precious cat mauling a nest of baby birds. I angrily shooed him away, picked the birds up off the ground and gingerly placed them back in their nest. My dad shouted, "Brenda, leave them alone! They'll probably just die anyway." Of course, the humanitarian in me wouldn't listen. I smuggled them into my bedroom and went back outside to dig up worms once it was dark. Then I stayed up half the night trying to nurse them back to health. I finally fell asleep from exhaustion around 2 a.m. When I awoke the next day, they were dead. I felt so guilty, as though somehow I had failed these helpless, frail creatures. For days afterwards, I could not hold my cat. When he came to me for love, I shunned him. This was an epiphany in my young life. I realized you could love something immensely but choose to discard it. Unbeknownst to me, this was an unsettling glimpse into my future.

Snuggling with Mac at 11 years old.

When it came to animals, I was always a softie. Every stray dog or cat that came our way pulled at my heartstrings. If a starving animal appeared on our doorstep, I begged my father to let me offer it some food. He'd always say, "You know, if you do, it'll want to stay!" Of course, *that* was my plan all along. I appealed to the protector in him and pled my case to keep them. Dad usually agreed because, despite outward appearances, he was a softie too. But he made it clear that if I didn't take care of them they'd starve to death; he had no intention of looking after them. Although this sounds pretty harsh, at the time I understood that this was my father's way of teaching me responsibility.

Caring for the animals in winter was particularly difficult. I'd make several trips to feed our dogs, tied up about fifty yards away. Sometimes the snow in the yard came up to my waist, and it was a struggle for me to carry a gallon of water in one hand and food and flashlight in the other hand and still maintain my balance. I was terribly afraid of the dark and what might lurk in those woods. As the moonlight beamed an eerie glow on the branches overhead, my heart and mind raced. Still, I forged ahead and faced my fears.

One night I did forget to feed my dogs. When I remembered the next day, my heart sank. I relived their hunger in my mind, imagining every hour that ticked by, empathizing with how they must have felt when they realized dinner wasn't coming that evening. As I raced to them, I wondered how they had even slept that night with aching, empty bellies. Had my absent-mindedness killed them? My father's warning that they would starve to death if I didn't feed them rang in my ears. They weren't dead, of course, just terribly ravenous. Of course, I ensured that they received double portions of food that night. Still, the anxiety I felt was so traumatic that nightmares haunted me years later. Little did I know that this anxiety would resurface later in my life but, tragically, it would be a *child* who starved, not an animal.

I lost some of my innocence and carefree spirit shortly after my ninth birthday. My teenage cousin (Tom's sister) caught Tom, Punchy, Deanna and me in the barn poking each other's genitals with straw. We were just naturally curious, and as an adult reflecting back I realize there was really no need to overreact. But I will never forget the sight of Deanna's mother grabbing her by the hair and whipping her with a leather belt repeatedly. Her cries reverberated over the rolling hills, her mother screaming and tugging forcefully on her arm, with strap in hand, still whipping her as she rounded the corner towards home. Even though I had seen my brother and sister get the belt (rarely) when they misbehaved, this was different. I honestly thought Deanna's mother wanted to kill her because the behavior seemed so violent, so inhumane. Watching Deanna's mother abuse her was the first thing that began to strip away my innocence, not the sexual experimentation. It's ironic that the very thing Deanna's mother tried to prevent (i.e., children growing up too fast) was the very thing she forced us to do.

My punishment, although not corporal, was quite shameful. I was forced to sit on the couch and tell my mother and older cousin exactly what we had done and why. It was utterly humiliating. The outline of the bathroom window nearby kept popping into my mind as a potential escape route. I imagined slipping through it quietly and just running away. Of course, I didn't know where I would go, but *anyplace* was better than where I was! I remember asking over and over again if I could use the bathroom. But, my suspicious mother wouldn't let me leave her sight. After a very excruciating interrogation that seemed to drag on forever, I was instructed to never play in the barn again with my cousins. (No more jumping from the hayloft!)

The next day, Deanna had bruising and rectangular welts all over her legs, and I struggled to understand why she'd been beaten but not I. It seemed very inequitable. I reasoned that her mother must not have loved her very much.

How could a "loving" mother hurt her child like that?[2]

Now, all parents accidentally hurt their children sometimes—you bounce them too high on your leg and they fall off, or you open a door into their nose—but most children are, fortunately, resilient and recognize that their parents didn't mean to injure them. However, it's the malicious willful assault on a child's emotional state or body, combined with a sense that the parent does not truly love him or her that causes a child to become scarred. Unfortunately, it doesn't take years of abuse for a parent to cause psychological damage. One isolated incident can traumatize a very young child.

There was a time a few years earlier that left an impression almost as indelible as the whipping Deanna received. My mother was driving our car into town with me in the middle of the front seat, sandwiched between my mother and sister. Cecile said something to my mother, who then reached across me with her arm and began smacking my sister in the mouth. Mother's elbow and forearm repeatedly struck me in the face. The car swerved, and we went off the road. Yes, I was frightened. But witnessing my sister's mouth fill with blood as her braces cut her lips and veering off the road wasn't what frightened me the most. My most terrifying memory was seeing my mother lose control. I knew in my heart that I would never subject my child to this out-of-control behavior.

The word "discipline" comes from the word "disciple." A disciple is someone who embraces the teachings of another.

---

[2] Years later I learned that Deanna had shot and killed her husband. He too had been beating her. She spent several years in prison, but was eventually released. Part of me can't help but wonder: If Deanna had been shown a little more love and a lot less leather would her life choices—indeed, her very life—have been any different?

Parents naturally want to teach (discipline) their rambunctious child(ren). They want to show them how to exhibit self-control and orderliness. Still, how can any parent *that* out of control teach self-control to his or her child?

Unbeknownst to me, my mother was about to transform from a woman out of control into something at the opposite end of the spectrum. She was about to become a subtly programmed robot, losing all independent thought and spontaneous emotion.

Even as a young child I always felt I was an old soul in a young person's body. I grew up very quickly, both emotionally and physically. Most people can't put a finger on when they started to grow up, but I can. It was the summer of 1971 when Hell, in all its fury, knocked on our front door. I was nine years old.

Chapter 3: Wolves in Sheep's Clothing

The greatest enemy of individual freedom is the individual himself.

Saul Alinsky

Jehovah's Witnesses (JWs) visited our home one otherwise fine summer day soliciting a free home Bible study. My mother, a Methodist Sunday school teacher, naively assumed that they could help her learn more about *her* God, never realizing she was about to receive instruction about *their* God, Jehovah. The Witnesses promptly informed us that our entire family needed to participate in the study. This raised a level of suspicion within me. My mother was the one who wanted to be well versed in the Bible. Why did the rest of the family need to become involved? My father and I were less than enthusiastic about the prospect of being pulled into their indoctrination, but in hindsight I understand that this is how the organization snares the entire family in the net. JWs know that a family divided can weaken their grip.

Like cattle being led blindly to slaughter, we all studied their literature (not the Bible) and started attending five weekly meetings. My poor father never anticipated the brainwashing our family would receive.

At first I enjoyed all the attention the nice Elder[3] and his wife gave our family. My initial enjoyment was very short-lived. I felt increasingly lost. Their cult-like, uniquely crafted vocabulary went right over my head, and quite frankly, I couldn't see the logic in most of their teachings.

The Kingdom Hall (i.e., church) that we attended was quite simplistic. It was a uniformly square building with only one small meeting space and two gender-appropriate bathrooms located in the rear. There were no intricately carved wooden pews or any beautiful stained-glass windows. In fact, there wasn't a single window in the whole building! Stepping inside produced a sense of claustrophobia, a feeling of being entombed. I spent most of my time daydreaming during services or fidgeted continuously in my seat in order to survive the repetitive religious banter. I was nevertheless able to digest certain bits of information—things a nine-year old child should *not* hear. I learned that someday "worldly people" (what JWs call all nonbelievers) might take my mother from me as part of our persecution. I was bombarded with this fear, along with other horrific tales. One such shocking story involved some captors rubbing salt into the wounds of a Jehovah's Witness after she had been beaten and gang raped.

Several Elders in our congregation had gone to prison, usually for failing to follow the laws of the land (e.g., serve in war, salute the flag, etc.). They'd too share, in graphic detail, the brutality they had endured. I sensed that recanting their

---

[3] An Elder is considered a leader in the Jehovah's Witness faith, and the man is considered the head of the household. Women are expected to be submissive to their husbands and are *not* permitted to be promoted within the organization or even pray aloud without having something covering their head. Ironically, although women are usually the driving force behind their family's paying homage, they have little recognized power within the organization.

horrors time and again made them feel more spiritually enlightened. The congregation so admired them for enduring these atrocities in the "name of Jehovah." Although I was exposed to these stories of abuse as a child, I found it absurd that I wasn't allowed to watch most television shows—especially police dramas—if there was even a hint of violence in the program. Mother could not begin to grasp the correlation that I saw so clearly.

The two or three hours I spent trying to sit perfectly still were, in my mind, equivalent to being tied to an anthill. It took all the strength I had in that little body of mine not to start screaming aloud with frustration. I was, in a sense, beginning to relate to the torture conveyed in our meetings. Most Christian religions instruct youngsters (who naturally have a limited attention span) using child-appropriate materials. Conversely, Jehovah's Witnesses don't believe in treating children as children. Children just one and two years old are expected to sit stoically in their seats and absorb information at the same intellectual level as adults. If going to the Kingdom Hall three times a week wasn't grueling enough, we started attending assemblies where thousands would gather and listen to sermon after sermon for eight hours or more, usually for three to five days in succession. Talk about a...g...o...n...i...z...i...n...g!

Our family's typical pose during meetings: On the left is my father, arms crossed, about to fall asleep. I'm on the right (age 11), leaning forward, trying to endure the torture of sitting on those hard plastic seats for two-plus hours, and in the middle sits my mother, head tilted, engrossed.

At the age of nine, I began writing some of my thoughts in my first diary. Journaling helped diffuse some of the rage igniting inside me.

After a few months of brainwashing, Mother was hooked. She unilaterally decided that our entire family needed to be baptized. However, my dad and I were less than enthusiastic. It just felt wrong. On the other hand, my brother and sister seemed to never give it a second thought.

My mother initially presented baptism to me as my decision, but that was really a façade to mask her intended manipulation of me. Before the highly anticipated event, she explained that if I didn't get baptized with them, I would have to get baptized *all by myself* later. I didn't know what being baptized involved, but I knew that I, a ten year old, didn't want to have to do it *alone,* nor did I want to stand before thousands of people in a bathing suit during puberty. (I had just started my period that year and was extremely self-conscious about my body.) It became obvious to me that this was my fate, not my choice. So there we were—my mother, sister, brother and I—being submerged into a swimming pool, never knowing that this single event would adversely alter our family dynamics forever. I didn't understand that baptism was a signed-in-blood contract. Baptism meant I was expected to devote the rest of my life to serving Jehovah, and there would be dire consequences if I failed. Once you became a JW, unlike the military, you'd never leave honorably. My dad's steadfastness in refusing to be baptized was a decision that later proved to be a blessing in disguise for both of us.

Why did my mother immerse herself and her children in this religion when she already had a Christian upbringing? I believe that my mother was a spiritual wasteland, looking for a higher purpose to her life, and perhaps seeking a community that would embrace her. She had been a full-time housewife and mother for over twenty years and was probably lonely. That combined with her limited experiences outside the home prevented her from making an educated, informed decision about what she was getting herself into. Hers was an emotional decision, not an intellectual one.

Over the next few months my mother set out to rescue every soul she met. Her attention turned to her immediate family—her mother, brothers, sister, and their children. Like a hurricane, she alienated everyone in her wake, and I remember more than one heated discussion with her brother, a Christian minister. They'd fire scriptures at each other, he using the King James Bible and she using the Jehovah's Witnesses' version. (Yes, Jehovah's Witnesses have their own Bible but insist that the content's meaning wasn't altered from the King James Bible during the translation process.) After a few hours, he would leave all flustered with Mother gloating that she got the best of him because she knew the scriptures better than he.

My maternal grandmother, Laura, had always been a very religious woman. When she was just fifteen, she married a farmer and together they raised eleven children. Gram was a petite fireball—very much like me—but loving and kind. As she hummed Bible hymns throughout the day, her optimistic spirit and joy for life rubbed off on me. I always felt better after spending some time with her and felt we were kindred spirits. When my mother would tell her own mother that she was in Satan's organization (despite the fact that she devoted her entire life to the Lord), it sure didn't sit well. As religious differences drove a wedge between the two, we stopped visiting my grandmother (other than to occasionally preach to her). I was, of course, heartbroken. (Down the road, however, my loving grandma would recognize my vulnerability and come to my aid. After her death, we would reunite on levels unimaginable, as you will soon see.)

Insulting our immediate family wasn't enough. We were expected to show all the pagans (i.e, every non-Jehovah's Witness) the error of their ways. Our strategy was not unlike any good salesperson's modus operandi. We surreptitiously made our way into as many homes as we could, turning on fountains of charisma and grinning from ear to ear. The men wore respectable suits and ties and the women, dresses. Thus, we never appeared threatening.

Once inside, we'd usually focus on a featured article of one of the Witnesses' *Awake* or *Watchtower* magazines. Our mission was considered successful if we were able to "place" a magazine with the resident for a "contribution." We were instructed to never use the word "sell." (Years later I learned that this policy helped the organization avoid paying taxes.) Those who were receptive were labeled "sheep." Those who were standoffish were labeled "goats."

We offered young people hope and the lonely and elderly companionship. JWs tapped into people's fears by talking about the crime rate, pollution, poverty and illness—i.e., everything is incredibly bleak—and then offered them a chance to **never** die, to be free of all these things. Outwardly, we appeared loving and deeply concerned about their lives. But behind their backs we viewed them as a contagious disease, satanic, and a populace to avoid (except to preach to them).

Even as a young child, I remember perceiving Jehovah's Witnesses as terribly judgmental and self-righteous. They condemned the rest of the world who had not found "The Truth," which is the term they used to define their religion. However, I always thought of it as "their truth."

The Elders controlled us by drilling the fear of death at Armageddon (Judgment Day, the end of the world as we know it) into our minds. If you didn't log enough hours or weren't zealous enough, although labeled a "Jehovah's Witness," you too might meet your end. And the problem is, you never knew what Jehovah considered adequate dedication, so you lived in a state of perpetual anxiety. Fortunately, I only believed Armageddon existed during the first two years of my indoctrination. Once I turned thirteen, I began to see this religion as one of gloom-and-doom and falsehood.

The last thing I want to do is preach to you about what Jehovah's Witnesses believe. After all, I have spent the last thirty years trying to deprogram myself. But I think it is important that you have a basic understanding of their religious philosophy—what makes them tick—just in case you have not had the distinct pleasure of their company in your home. If you would like further information on the background and theology of the religion, you might want to do an Internet search. Once you do, you will find links to their headquarters (the Watchtower Bible and Tract Society);

numerous books written by former members; and countless support groups for ex-Witnesses who are in all stages of emotional recovery.

Jehovah's Witnesses believe Jehovah will destroy all nonbelievers and that only *they* will be left after Armageddon. Jehovah, their loving God, will even murder innocent babies and young children if their parents are not baptized. Any day now, you and your entire family will die if you don't join their ranks, give up your "worldly" (non-believing) ways, and become a devout JW. Imagine how frightening this belief, if embraced, would be to an adult, let alone a child! Fear is a powerful motivator to coerce conformity.

I distinctly remember *one* of the years when JWs said this annihilation was going to happen—1975. (They've predicted many other dates as well.) Some Jehovah's Witnesses sold their homes to become more active in door-to-door service or put off dental work with the anticipation that the end was near. Higher education was discouraged because vocational goals were not considered necessary in the "New Order." (As a result, my brother dropped out of college.)

When Armageddon didn't come to fruition in 1975, the Watchtower Bible and Tract Society announced that the time for the great event would be of God's choosing, conveniently clouding their prediction that 1975 was ever the target date. They even blamed their failed prophecy on their own members, saying, "...it was not the word of God that failed or deceived him and brought disappointment, but that his own understanding was based on wrong premises." (Watchtower, July 15, 1976, p. 441) (In my opinion, either Jehovah likes to be made a fool of, or JWs are false prophets! Wouldn't almighty God get it right the first time?)

They now refer to their frequent changes in policy as "new light" handed down to them by Jehovah. (I've always been curious about how this "new light" comes to them. In this modern age, could it be transmitted by telefax, phone, or e-mail?) They'd assure you that God's spirit directs them as they are God's sole channel of communication. Yet, curiously, if anyone else made this claim, the Governing Body (the Watchtower leadership in New York) would say Satan the Devil is directly communicating with that person.

After Armageddon, each person for the next "x" number of years will be expected to dispose of the bones of the millions who were slain. Once this grisly task is accomplished, the remaining Jehovah's Witnesses will live in peace on Earth for about one thousand years, completely safe from the influence of Satan, now bound and powerless. After one thousand years, Jehovah will free Satan—once again—to tempt the sinners. Every JW who survived the first annihilation will then undergo a second loyalty test. A final slaughter will take place when Jehovah weeds out the truly devout Jehovah's Witnesses from the semi-devout. (Leave no doubt, my mother definitely falls into the devout category.) After Satan has fulfilled his duty, he'll be permanently destroyed. The survivors will then worship and serve Jehovah, their God of love, for eternity.

Even as a young child, I quite frankly had a lot of trouble understanding the appeal of this kind of future. I mean, who in their right mind would want to pick up rotting, dead bodies for years, then endure an eternity of servitude? Not me! Unlike most of my family, I was able to spot the loose bricks in the foundation.

According to Christian doctrine, a fiery Hell awaits all sinners. But for Jehovah's Witnesses, Hell is the grave. So technically, everyone eventually goes to Hell when they die, even Jehovah's Witnesses. The nuance of that connotation (JWs going to Hell) makes me chuckle. I wonder if they have ever thought of that? My usually pessimistic dad said once, "Hell is what we live right here on Earth as we struggle day to day!" (Perhaps as you continue to read my story and reflect on your own battles, you'll find some truth in that statement.)

On the other hand, Jehovah's Witnesses *do* believe in heaven. But according to them, only 144,000 lucky souls—the cream of the crop—will make it there. The exactness of this number, which they claim is foretold in the Bible, suggests that Jehovah has already preordained (an airtight fate for some zealots) who will be selected. So what happens to those who joined the organization *after* the 144,000 were chosen? Does this mean that Mr. Smith next door is out of luck despite his belief that he belongs to a heavenly class? Yes, it does. Where's the logic? Here are a few other things with which I took issue:

(1) Why does salvation only apply to Jehovah's Witnesses? The religion wasn't founded until 1876 by a mortal man, Charles Taze Russell. So, what about the millions of people who served God prior to Russell? Are they going to be left on the sidelines simply because they happened to be born before the organization was founded? What about Christ's disciples? Wouldn't it be reasonable to assume that they'd rank near the top of the list of candidates for eternal life? Yet, they called themselves, "Jesus' disciples." They didn't call themselves "Jehovah's Witnesses." Would this discrepancy penalize them?

Never fear. Jehovah's Witnesses seem to have all the answers: Anyone who lived *before* the organization was founded will be resurrected at Armageddon to hear "The Truth" (i.e., their religious beliefs). If these individuals who have been brought back from the dead decline to become Jehovah's Witnesses, then Jehovah will ensure that they get to experience death *a second time.* I see a major problem with this grandiose scenario: How is the

Earth going to support the billions of people who've inhabited this planet since the dawn of time? Sounds like standing room only to me!

(2) If Jesus died for us a long time ago so we could be forgiven for our sins, what is the purpose of releasing Satan to tempt us all over again? Doesn't that negate Jesus' sacrifice? Does Jehovah really need to release Satan to get us to sin again? Why can't Jehovah be satisfied with the Armageddon survivors' devotion? In my book, all those years spent picking up dead bodies should count for something!

(3) If God wanted us to come to know him through Jehovah's Witnesses, why did he wait until the late 1800s to create this organization? Why weren't JWs, as they are known, out preaching door to door thousands of years ago?

(4) And why would Satan, knowing full well that he is going to be destroyed eventually, work hand in hand with God to tempt people after being chained for one thousand years? Would you kiss the boots of someone you knew was going to stomp out your existence? Wouldn't you just say, "Up yours and get it over with!" Are we to assume that Satan is clueless about Jehovah's plot to eliminate him after one thousand years but that mere humans (the JWs) are privy to this information?

(5) Why would God murder innocent children just because they had parents who chose not to sign up for a particular religion? Is their loving God that cold-hearted and unmerciful? What a contradiction!

My dad, who only completed eighth grade, used to wisely articulate, "Common sense is not so common." I agree. Where is the common sense in this religion?

Before I became a Witness, I relished sleeping in on Saturday mornings. When I finally did crawl out of bed, I leisurely absorbed my favorite cartoons. Becoming a Jehovah's Witness changed all that. Every weekend, without fail, we'd have to wake up quite early so we could meet at the Kingdom Hall to map out the territory we would "work" for the rest of the day. But to me it meant going door-to-door to preach something that I didn't believe in. We called it "witnessing" or "going out in service." Most people would simply say, "I'm not interested," which never seemed to deter my mother. If she felt especially belligerent that day, she'd brazenly push open their door as they attempted to close it. "*You* aren't interested in God?" she'd sneer. Funny thing is, they would always get a wee bit nastier after that.

On one occasion, an obscenity-shouting homeowner actually unleashed his growling dogs on us. Luckily, I was carrying a big briefcase filled with literature, which protected my exposed legs as I backed into the car. Conversely, sometimes lonely old widows took pity on us, offering us something to drink when it was unbearably hot, or allowing us to step inside when it was bitterly cold. Those kind souls were a blessing; they helped me realize that there were good people in "the world." Everyone wasn't as evil as the JWs wanted me to believe.

The weather was never a hindrance. We'd make our appointed rounds (always with exposed legs—females were never allowed to wear pants) whether it was 100°F or −10°F. In Pennsylvania, the humidity can cut through you like a razor in the winter and turn you into a cesspool in the summer. But we were expected to put in our monthly allotment of hours no matter what. The Elders kept track of our time, and Jehovah's Witnesses who didn't fulfill their quotas were admonished, shamed and counseled.[4] There was little to no time in the Jehovah's Witness' day for recreation or vacations. On brutally cold winter days, I'd hobble home, prop my extremities in front of the heater vent and wait patiently for the furnace to kick on. Once it did, the painful burn consumed my frozen flesh as it slowly thawed.

When I wasn't in school during the summer, my mother signed us up to "pioneer," which meant each of us was expected to go preaching about a hundred hours each month. Every week I (a child!) was expected to put in twenty-five hours of service work, *plus* six hours of meetings, two to four hours of home Bible studies (our family held their own study in addition to the usual Kingdom Hall meetings) and several hours of personal study and talk preparation. (Female Witnesses were expected to rehearse proselytizing in front of the entire congregation by role-playing how to overcome objections from people.) If you tabulate my enslavement, that's about forty hours of religious activity every week! I angrily resented giving up my time, my life, to a cause that seemed so ludicrous.

What most people don't realize is that Jehovah's Witnesses keep track of any and all interaction with you (the "householder") after they come to your home. (They do this even when they interject something scriptural to you, their relative, during casual conversation.). Every person remotely interested was documented in some way. Those who appeared to be somewhat receptive to our spiel were referred to as "back calls" (i.e., call back on this person) and would be visited again soon—very soon. Anyone who purchased, or even accepted "free" literature, was instantly labeled a back

---

[4] I believe many JWs go out preaching not so much to save others from damnation but to simply log hours so they can appease the organization and ultimately survive when Armageddon arrives. When you think about it, their motives are purely selfish and fear-based, but I doubt few of them ever look closely enough to see their true reflection in the mirror.

call. Moral of the story: If you *don't* want Jehovah's Witnesses back on your doorstep within a few weeks, reject anything they offer you.

It didn't take long to learn that certain houses in each territory were off limits because a "disfellowshipped" person lived there. I didn't know what that word meant, but I knew it was A BAD THING (more about this later). I'd carefully circumvent these homes to keep the evil inside from harming me. When I too became one of those alleged evildoers, I learned that disfellowshipped was a powerful word to throw around. Nothing would get an unsuspecting Jehovah's Witness off my doorstep faster than brandishing the "D" word!

All kidding aside, I came to realize that my fear of being shot by a rifle-slinging nonbeliever or attacked by a pack by dogs was incidental compared to my real trepidation at the time—knocking on the door of a fellow classmate or teacher and being known as a "Jehovah's Witness."

Chapter 4: Keep Paddling

Although this chapter discusses abuse, it is not so much about paddling in the physical sense of the word as it is about trying to row upstream against the emotional currents that we face in life. I spent almost ten years in an emotional prison paddling religiously (pun intended) to stay afloat. I lived alone in places only a former cult member, someone who walked a mile in my service shoes, could truly understand.

The most ravaging storm of my young life blew in when I was just ten years old, and it whipped me around with such ferocity that my world spun out of control for the next decade. Mother, with a credulous, somber expression on her face, sat me down and informed me that I was <u>never</u> to speak to anyone who wasn't a Jehovah's Witness again. Can you imagine how you would feel if some organization waltzed into your life and demanded that you cut off all associations with your friends and relatives—that you never even say "hello" to them again?

Up until then, my social life revolved around my cousins, and I looked forward to family reunions each summer with my grandmother, cousins, aunts and uncles. Sure, I felt anger. But as children often do, I blamed myself. My anger took a back seat to the guilt that consumed me. I reasoned: If I hadn't been so sexually curious during the incident in the barn, maybe this wouldn't be happening.

Like an abusive husband who isolates his wife from others in order to control her, Jehovah's Witnesses use isolation to control "the flock" (i.e., their members). As a full-fledged, baptized Jehovah's Witness, you are admonished to avoid worldly people at all costs, unless you are trying to convert them. Any friendships you cultivate must be with those in The Truth.

In time I learned that in addition to losing my cousins, I was forfeiting all future friendships. For in our rural congregation, there was no one even remotely close to my age. Not one JW friend existed for me. Although I had done nothing wrong, I was being grounded for the next nine years.

Earlier that same year my sister informed me that there was no Santa Claus (after I went snooping into my parents' closet and found a not-so-well-concealed Barbie doll). Like most youngsters, I was surprised and a bit disappointed, but in my heart, Santa was not what Christmas was about anyway. What was more important to me was the excitement of helping my mom open the storage box containing our artificial Christmas tree. The silver branches made a crisp rustling sound as we took turns extracting them from each plain, brown paper wrapper. I looked forward to decorating the tree with lights, smelling the scent of cinnamon in the air and watching mom spread flour all over the rectangular-shaped, metal kitchen table where she rolled out cookie and pie dough. It was the *feeling* that Christmas invoked that was so special, not the fact that some fat man slid down a chimney. Even with Santa officially gone, we could still have our traditions, right? Wrong!

Then the second wave of news hit: We would no longer celebrate Christmas. For that matter, we wouldn't celebrate any holiday—Easter, Thanksgiving, Valentine's Day, Independence Day, Mother's Day, Father's Day. I felt mortified as I watched my mother throw out our family's Christmas tree and ornaments. I desperately wanted to save my childhood memories from the trash. My father balked, "Why can't we just donate the tree and ornaments to a needy family?" "No!" mother responded. Christmas was a pagan holiday. She couldn't possibly give demonic items to someone else! Christmas came and went that year like any other day. While everyone in the world rejoiced, I wept.

Have you ever heard the saying, "Bad news comes in threes?" Well, she wasn't done yet. *We would never celebrate my birthday again.* No more sleepovers, no more presents, no more parties, no affirmation that I was loved and wanted on this, my special day. To this day, I still can't tell you in what month or year my family members were born or how old they are because no one ever discussed it.

At nine I had friends, relatives and holidays to celebrate life. At ten, I lost everything dear. All the goodness in my life was replaced with bitter emptiness.

After the storm subsided, I found myself speeding down an incline on a roller coaster. You know the nauseating feeling you get when your stomach seems to levitate and panic starts to set in right before the roller coaster levels out? For me, the roller coaster never leveled out and never stopped dropping. Every morning I awoke feeling emotionally and physically sick. With my sense of security pulled out and no desire to live in the present, I had no choice but to look to the future for solace.

My cousins who used to play with me late into the evening now felt snubbed because I couldn't even acknowledge them. If they rode their bikes past our house and yelled, "Hi, Brenda," I had to ignore them and turn tail without responding. I felt so ashamed of who I was ("a Jehovah") but so fearful that if I even said "hello" to them, I would be punished. My cousins' prejudices began to reflect those of their parents who obviously criticized my mother, but it was I who felt their disapproval. As a child, I felt I needed to defend our religious beliefs, even though I did not agree with them. Outwardly, I began to live a double life.

I always dreaded the first day of school as a Jehovah's Witness because my mother always showed up to ensure my teacher understood the JW rules: no holiday participation, no school activities, no saluting the flag. (When all the children stood, I had to stay seated in my chair and keep my mouth shut. Of course, I stuck out like Pinocchio's nose! Children glared at me, pointed and whispered behind my back.) During holiday parties, my mother removed me from the celebration just as it began. It was frustrating to watch my teacher hand out the goodies, knowing I couldn't even get a morsel of a cookie. When the class list was sent home for Valentine's Day, my classmates were instructed to make cards for everyone, except me. I received no birthday acknowledgments, Thanksgiving feast, Christmas presents or chocolate Easter candy. After my mother pointed out how our religion was radically different, she'd leave some literature and try to set up an appointment, hoping to further indoctrinate my teacher with her beliefs. This routine continued year after year. Most teachers were tolerant; others became downright abusive—to me.

As we all know, children can be cruel to others who seem different from them. But as a young child, I learned adults could be far crueler. One teacher in particular comes to mind. He was a respected minister, a sadist, actually, who enjoyed paddling me during my fifth grade year. This was no miniscule paddle; it was about two feet long with holes drilled in it! Right before class ended, he'd force me to the front of the classroom and have me face the chalkboard so he could give me a few malicious whacks, not because I had done something wrong, but because he (erroneously) saw me as a Jehovah's Witness. As I fought to hold back the tears, it wasn't really the physical blows that hurt the most, it was the humiliation and sense of betrayal that consumed me. I still distinctly remember the smile that was frozen on my teacher's face as he ordered me to turn around and face the chalkboard.

After a few days of this abuse, I realized his fun had just begun and that I better "tattletale" on my teacher, even if it made him mad. As any child would do, I sought refuge from my mother. Her subsequent comment left me aghast and confused. She nonchalantly replied, "Brenda, persecution is good. It shows we are in the right religion. You shouldn't hate this man, but rather dislike his ways." Powerless to do anything else, I continued into class to receive my daily dose of persecution from this so-called religious leader. I couldn't help but feel like one of those frail baby birds I had tried to rescue. Like my cat, my teacher had become a predator. The difference, however, was that no one was trying to save me. My mother's maternal instinct to protect her own seemed to have vanished. *That* hurt me worse than the paddling I endured.

A few years later, I collided with the wrath of another teacher who detested Jehovah's Witnesses. Every day, I walked quietly into his classroom, sat down at my desk, and stared straight ahead until all the children had noisily filed into the classroom. And every day as soon as the classroom quieted down, the teacher looked at me and announced authoritatively, "Brenda—in the corner!" After several weeks, my grades (mostly As) plummeted. Mother eventually questioned my declining grades. I told her I couldn't see the chalkboard or take any notes; my nose was literally pressed to the wall every day. When she confronted the teacher and asked why I was sitting in the corner every day, he could offer no explanation, even admitting that I had done nothing wrong. My mother suggested that I be allowed to return to my desk. He complied without incident, probably thankful that she didn't bring the matter before the principal or school board first. (She should have!)

Classmates could be equally cruel, and I was frequently bullied. One group of girls waited eagerly each day for the bell to ring, then they'd run up behind me in the hallway and shove me into the wall as hard as they could, chanting, "Hey, Jehovah." I always responded like a good little Jehovah's Witness girl by "turning the other cheek." But after several weeks, the abuse became unbearable. I turned around and grabbed the ringleader by the shirt, slammed *her* against the wall and yelled, "If you ever touch me again, I'll kill you!" After that, she and her hoard of friends didn't lay a hand on me (although they continued to hurl verbal insults when the opportunity arose). For the average child, this would solve one's problem, but not for me. For the next few months I struggled not with physical assaults but with emotional ones. I feared that my mother and/or the Elders might find out about my aggression and reprimand me for defending myself; after all, I was expected to never "bring reproach upon Jehovah's name" as a JW child. This self-induced guilt is precisely why I handled the next incident very differently.

My next tormentor made his appearance on my daily bus ride home. A neighbor boy took delight in walloping me on the head with his three-inch-thick history book. Since my skull was pretty thick, I could usually cope with the dizziness and headache that ensued. However, one day as I tried desperately to sneak past him and slink down into my seat, he hit me so hard that the impact gave me a black and blue eye. I didn't tell my mother what happened, and she never asked. (After all, we both knew persecution was good for me.) However, when my dad got home from work that night and saw my swollen eyelid, he became enraged. We drove over to the neighbor's house and my usually soft-spoken father had a few choice words with the boy's father. After spouting a few expletives I'd never heard before, my dad threatened to call the police and have the father thrown in jail if it happened again.

You probably wonder why I didn't go to my father immediately when my mother wouldn't stand up to the teacher who paddled me. The explanation is simple: I knew my mother was a formidable force in our household. Although my father was deemed head of the household by the religion's standards, mother actually ruled the roost. I doubted whether my own father would be allowed to contradict her, especially when it came to persecution. (A woman who has an unbelieving husband is supposed to "accept his headship" *except* if he prevents her from attending religious meetings, preaching door to door, or instructing her children in the faith.) I wanted to reach out to him more, but I knew if I did and he didn't help me, it would double my emotional pain and distrust. Psychologists call this secondary wounding.

Although I was embarrassed to be paraded before this boy and his father, I admired and respected my father for taking a stand on my behalf. After this incident, I realized that my father truly did care about me. Interestingly enough, although I suffered bouts of physical abuse while attending school, unlike most children, I actually looked forward to school. It was an emotional and social outlet from the continuous isolation I experienced at home.

While abuse of children (both in and out of this religion) hasn't ceased to exist, fortunately, it's more widely talked about and, in some societies, a little less tolerated. But people today still turn their backs on children, especially Jehovah's Witness children. In addition to persecution by the outside world, many children are subjected daily to emotional, sexual and physical abuse by their own Jehovah's Witness parents.

Offenders (oftentimes Elders or even higher ranking officials) who abuse either their wives or their children are questioned by the Elders, and the matter is typically dropped. Members are frequently instructed to keep such matters from authorities (lest it reflect poorly on the organization's reputation). It's a twisted, pathetic system that perpetuates abuse within its confines. Unfortunately, it's the innocent children who suffer the most.

When I was twelve years old, my nineteen-year-old sister married a Jehovah's Witness, and one year later she delivered a beautiful baby boy. From the time Jon was old enough to walk, he adoringly followed me everywhere. I called him my shadow, and when I did, he giggled hysterically and repeated back to me in his gleeful innocence, "I'm Brenna's shadow!" A simple task such as going to the bathroom proved to be no small feat; Jon moaned and pleaded for me outside the door until I emerged. Jon gave my dreary teenage life purpose. I adored him.

During summer break I sometimes spent a week visiting my sister. She lived about sixty miles away, and although she was a JW, she didn't seem to live and breathe the religion as stringently as my mother. With her, I could have a conversation that didn't include scripture. We'd talk about "normal" stuff, and I'd help her clean house and make supper, giving her the rare break she needed from running after a toddler.

Sadly, Jon would come to know at a tender age of one the frustration I experienced sitting on that anthill during those long sermons in the Kingdom Hall. Since there wasn't a Sunday school atmosphere at these meetings, young children weren't allowed to amuse themselves with toys or coloring books. When Jon started fidgeting, I did everything in my power to try to keep him still, e.g., allowing him to forage through the makeup in my purse, digging trenches into it with his fingernails to amuse himself. I sacrificed my necklaces as a distraction. When I ran out of tricks and could no longer contain his energy, his father grabbed him by the arm and literally dragged him to the restroom to beat him. Jon's beating became such a ritual that when his daddy reached for him during a meeting, he knew it meant a beating. He cried and pleaded "No, Daddy" as he buckled his legs, refusing to walk willingly to meet his fate.

Everyone in the Kingdom Hall could hear his screams. The sound that echoed from the blow varied; sometimes Jon's father used his hand, sometimes a belt. After ten or fifteen minutes, they would return with Jon hyperventilating, desperately trying to catch his breath. Beaten into composure, he would sit still for a while longer. Usually he stared motionless into space, his eyes bloodshot from crying. If fate smiled on him, Jon fell asleep in my arms for the duration of the meeting. If not, then back again to the restroom he would go for another beating and the cycle continued, until the closing prayer.

It broke my heart. I wanted desperately to stop the abuse, but I was a child myself and didn't know what to do to save him, or me. His was not an isolated incident. Sometimes there was literally a line to the restrooms so that children could receive their punishment for displaying natural restlessness during these incredibly tedious meetings.

One heart-wrenching day in particular is forever seared into my memory. My sister confided in my mother, father, and me that Jon, then two years old, had asked his father to hit him on his hands with the belt instead of his buttocks. When asked why he wanted to be punished that way, he replied, "Because my butt is too sore." It sickened all of us. But none of the adults—my sister, my mother nor my father— did anything about it. And the Witnesses seemed to condone it with the "spare the rod and spoil the child" scripture. Within a year, my sister had another child and his fate, sadly, was no different than Jon's. Meanwhile, my sister's husband was rewarded for his devotion to the faith. He was made an Elder.

As an adult much later, I learned that Jon and I weren't alone. (See www.silentlambs.org, a website dedicated to the thousands of abuse survivors within this organization.)

I knew in my heart that eventually I'd have to say good-bye and walk away from these helpless children in order to save myself, but the idea of self-preservation shredded my sense of loyalty. Still, I knew there was nothing I could do to help them—at least not until I helped myself. (In a later chapter, you'll see that I tried to help Jon when he became a young adult. I so desperately wanted to be there for him since I was unable to help him as a youngster. But the choices he'd make would ultimately cost him his freedom—and nearly his life.)

I had no misgivings about what happened to someone who left the faith. Many unbelievers were eventually disfellowshipped (excommunicated) from the congregation (whether or not they committed any sin) and disowned by their families, never to be spoken to again. Despite this knowledge, I felt I had no choice. If I left, I would live. If I stayed, I would die. Additionally, in my mind, I had nothing else to lose. My mother, sister, and brother symbolically died on that fateful summer day when that nice Elder and his wife knocked on our door. Although I entertained thoughts of suicide, I had no intention of allowing my spirit—my very life—to also wither away.

During my teenage years, I wasn't the type of child to rebel. Instead, I respectfully did all that my parents asked of me. On at least one occasion, however, I tried to test my mother to see if I had to follow her religious rules to the letter. I nonchalantly suggested that I stop attending meetings at the Kingdom Hall. My mother responded to my obvious dissension by getting an Elder into our home so he could witness to me for a very long time. (They call it "providing loving assistance.") The same "nice" Elder who converted my mother sat me down and assured me that Satan was influencing me for having any thoughts that deviated from Jehovah's teachings, and that I needed to obey my mother and serve Jehovah. In my heart, I didn't care one nanosecond about their beliefs; after all, they didn't care about mine. (I employed the wise, old adage: "Before you can be heard, you must first seek to understand.") However, I knew he would preach to me until I succumbed. So, after several hours of being psychologically bound to the couch, I lied and told him what he wanted to hear just so I could get away. Sounds like brainwashing, doesn't it? It was.

Now consider this double standard: Although I wasn't old enough in their minds to make a choice to stop attending meetings (or vote, wear makeup, drive a car, or get a tattoo), I was old enough (through baptism at age ten) to vow an allegiance to Jehovah forever.

It was about this time that outward symptoms of my profound distress began to show. The invisible restraints that held me in my seat at meetings for hours upon end were chafing away at my flesh. I reacted much like a captive animal chewing its leg off to free itself; I began biting my nails until they bled. The bloody stumps at the tips of my fingers kept me focused on something else besides the sermon and helped me escape. My parents encouraged me to stop gnawing away on myself, never understanding that I was manifesting a psychological trauma, not a physical one. I knew I was injuring myself, but I couldn't stop. When the nail became infected, I'd simply pierce the swollen flesh with a needle and squeeze the pus out to relieve the pressure. It was painful, but not nearly as painful as sitting through a meeting on that anthill.

Another method I developed to cope with the tedium during a lecture was to shift my weight and continuously squeeze my crossed legs together. This helped alleviate the mounting frustration and, consequently, I achieved my first orgasm. The orgasm relieved the stress for a while. Of course, after another thirty minutes or so of sitting rigidly, the stress would build up again. So I'd have another orgasm, then another. I have to laugh now to think that as the Jehovah's Witnesses were lecturing the congregation about the perils of masturbation and sex, I was having multiple orgasms! And amazingly, no one ever knew!

For three years, I wrote down my thoughts in a secretive diary, which I kept haphazardly hidden under my mattress. When I lost a baby tooth, I taped it into my diary. Since we didn't believe in the Tooth Fairy, it wouldn't do any good to put it under my pillow. This tooth collection was my attempt to hold onto the once happy childhood that was slipping through my fingers. Eventually, my sister and her best friend (also a Jehovah's Witness) found my diary and broke the lock. They threw away my baby teeth and ridiculed me for saving them. When I ran to my mother to complain about what they had done, she announced smugly that she too read my diary and didn't like a comment I'd made about her religion. According to Mother, I needed to change my attitude because Satan was influencing me. (Satan was influencing *me*? Which of her daughters broke into someone else's property and defaced it?) Once again, I felt so betrayed, so violated! Now my body wasn't the only thing being controlled sitting on that anthill in the Kingdom Hall; my intimate thoughts were being monitored and censored as well.

As I saw it, my choice was simple: find a way to keep journaling or kill myself. I knew I had to desperately hang onto the person inside who was being eroded away. The only way to do that was to protect my thoughts. I wrapped myself (my thoughts), in plastic and tucked me (my diary) away in an old, hollow log situated in a grove of trees. Every time I wanted to write, I'd go to the tranquility of the forest to release my anxiety. It's amazing the clever ideas a person can generate when backed into a corner! Still, the emotional assaults at home continued.

I coped with solitary confinement by creating a fantasy world with my Barbie dolls. The scenario was always the same: Ken married Barbie, they'd make love, then have a baby and live happily ever after. This fantasy world provided much comfort and joy. One day I came home from school to find my dolls gone. Mother had given them away. If my life could be likened to a puzzle, every day she seemed to remove another piece. How could she be so cruel? With my mother, the answers always came swiftly, "Now, maybe you'll read the *Watchtower* and *Awake* magazines more!" I refused to accept defeat, dwell on my loss, or succumb to her manipulation. I refused to become a victim! Instead, I changed the world within me and simply shifted my focus to something else: a fantasy life in Hollywood.

Weeks earlier, my mother informed me that I could keep the ten cents I earned for each religious magazine I sold. (Mother thought I would see this as an allowance, but even as a very young child I could see her real motive. The money was clearly just a bribe to coerce me to go preaching more.) Her motives aside, I knew if I saved my dimes for several weeks, I could afford to purchase entertainment magazines when I traveled to town with her.

Like most teens, celebrities intrigued me. I **dreamt** that someday I'd become a famous actress. Oh, to live a glamorous life where everyone would respect and admire me! Over the next two years, I collected several three-ring binders and filled them with memorabilia. Scrapbooking helped me endure many lonely hours. Most people would see this as simply a hobby. As usual, my mother had a different perspective: I was worshipping these celebrities and not Jehovah. (I beg to differ! Didn't I spend over one hundred hours studying and preaching door to door every month?)

Obviously, mother didn't see it that way because she demanded I burn my binders. For the first time, I took an unwavering stand. I clearly didn't worship this hobby, but it, like my Barbie dolls, had given my excessively religious existence some balance. I crossly informed her that if she made me destroy them I would **never** speak to her again. I don't think she was prepared for the storm I'd been brewing inside because she did back down and let me keep them. Thirty years later, I still have them today tucked away in a box in my basement. Each one represents a little piece of my sanity that stayed intact.

Privacy. What a concept! There was none in our household. From the day I was born, my sister and I shared a bedroom. When my sister got married and moved away, I looked forward to finally having the room to myself. Once again, my mother had other plans. She promptly moved into *my* bedroom, occupying the queen bed left vacant by my sister. Mother confided that she couldn't sleep with my restless father. Her explanation didn't seem viable; I knew better. My mother had fallen out of love with my father and in love with someone else. She had chosen instead a divine, perfect being: Jehovah. It was painfully obvious that her husband and children were no longer as important. (This is a common complaint among former Jehovah's Witness men.) Still, the Witnesses preach that a wife must fulfill her wifely duties. My mother obliged my father in that regard. Every now and then (about once a month or so) she'd announce, "Brenda, I'm going to go sleep with your father tonight." About ten minutes later she would quietly reappear in our room and climb back into bed. I found it utterly revolting to know that during that brief interlude my parents were having sex. At the same time, however, I found it amusing that she'd try to deceive me by tiptoeing back into bed. It reminded me of the teenager who sneaks in at night to avoid her parents (except the roles were reversed). So many times the oppressed, obnoxious teenager in me wanted to inquire, "Was it good for you? Ten minutes was awfully quick!" However, I remained silent because although I could see and feel her failure as both a wife and mother, it was just not in my nature to be disrespectful.

One of the ways I survived the frustration of losing all privacy was what I affectionately coined "silking." I'd take the silk on the end of a blanket and run the edge through my fingers, folding it in the process until I got to the other end. The cool silk was gratifying on a hot summer day. However, having my mother in my room was not only an invasion of my privacy, but it hindered me from giving myself the slightest bit of comfort. When I began silking, sometimes my mother heard the rustling of my blankets and asked me what I was doing. "Nothing," I'd reply, and immediately stop, feeling embarrassed. She no doubt thought I was "sinfully" masturbating. What ridiculous secrets we kept from each other!

Summer break was absolutely the worst time of the year for me. While other children looked forward to getting out of school so they could hang out with friends and forego homework, I dreaded it. For the most part, school was my sanctuary. Being at home in the summer meant ninety days of solitary confinement. Even though I was forbidden to have contact with anyone who was not a Jehovah's Witness, I took advantage of any free time I could while at school to chat with normal people. I became the essay queen. I got caught talking so much in study hall that I was assigned to write, "I will not talk in study hall" for nearly four months straight! (A small price to pay for social interaction.) Out of the reins of my mother, I had a circle of friends I loved and who loved me. It was heartbreaking to say good-bye to them every summer for three long months.

When home alone, I passed the time (when I wasn't performing my religious duties) by playing Monopoly—alone. Anyone for "Monopoly for One?" I would ask aloud. I would then set up the entire board—cards and money—and pretend I was the token car. Another token, perhaps the shoe, was my alter ego. For hours, I'd roll the dice for both players until someone won. Granted, I didn't become a split personality in the literal sense, but perhaps this was a close encounter. Although it was a pathetic existence, this simple board game served me well during those times of isolation.

Most experts recognize that developing close friendships is a necessary part of a teenager's development. My social development was irrevocably erased in order to fulfill the contract of the Jehovah's Witnesses. Consequently, I had many problems fitting in with society later as a young adult.

People often ask me why I think my sister and brother didn't seem to mind the restrictions imposed by Jehovah's Witnesses as much as I. What it boils down to is this: I had my friendships stripped away, whereas my sister and brother had very different social experiences. Because they were much older when we were baptized (my sister was seventeen and brother was twenty), unlike me they had been allowed to cultivate numerous friendships throughout their teen years.

For the next nine years, Mother reassured me that Jehovah would send me a Witness friend. My sister fed me the same empty assurances. According to them, I just had to be patient. Somehow Jehovah missed their prayers because it *never* happened.

By mid-summer of my sixth grade year, I was bored out of my mind and desperate to talk to *someone* my own age. I tiptoed to the phone and called my friend, Jaclyn, who lived less than two miles away. Quietly I whispered, "Meet me at the end of the lane." A few minutes later, I passed my mother in the kitchen and remarked that I was going outside to ride my bike. I peddled as fast as I could, uphill the whole way, to meet Jaclyn. I can't tell you how angelic she looked when my eyes saw her in the distance. My sagging spirit and heavy heart lifted with joy. I held back the tears as we hugged and exchanged a few words. A few minutes later I peered down the road and saw my mother driving towards us. She caught me! After the car skidded to an abrupt stop, Mother crossly scolded, "Get home right now!" Once home, she proceeded to reprimand me about having associations with unbelievers. From that day on, I was only permitted to ride my bike in front of our house. The walls were slowly but steadily closing in.

That summer crept by ever so slowly, and when it ended, I left elementary school, and Jaclyn, behind. The middle school I was about to attend was extremely old and depressing. I dreaded the thought of having to spend my days in such a dreary place (it resembled the school in the movie, *Matilda*—a movie I can readily relate to). However, within those four drab walls, I developed some amazing friendships that lasted decades. My friends were good people—scholastic, beautiful and respectful. They didn't smoke, use drugs or swear, but my mother saw them as undesirable and "worldly." (They would have been considered saints by any other mother's standards.) They knew the relationship I had with my family was tumultuous and as good friends, they really supported me. Every day the four or five of us spent our recess sharing our lives, talking about our teachers, our **hopes** and **dreams**, and boys—well, mostly boys. Oh, how I loved them all!

Sometime in eighth grade, I felt the noose around my neck getting a little too tight and my emotional state becoming unbearably fragile. I did something I'd never done before. I ditched several classes and spent three hours venting to a guidance counselor. It was also about this time that I wrote the short story, "All Alone in the World," in Chapter 1.

During those three hours with the counselor, one of my closest friends, Jennifer, sat beside me as my emotional right arm and clutched my hand in hers. She empathized as I tearfully relayed to the counselor how trapped, powerless and empty I felt. I spoke of how desperately I wanted to experience what the rest of my peers took for granted:

- To sleep over at a friend's house and stay up giggling half the night
- To participate in school functions (band, theater, choir, parties, dances, football games)
- To open Christmas and birthday presents
- To be allowed to date
- To just fit into society

I explained how I always made up something wonderful when teachers asked the class to share their Christmas gifts. I was just too ashamed to say I didn't get anything. I told her about the teacher who paddled me for weeks. I shared my plan to break free of the JW organization, but that I knew I'd have to wait until I was eighteen before I could legally flee. Even after spending three years of serving what amounted to a prison sentence, I was obligated to put in five more years of time before I could be released. There was no parole in sight for me, not even for perfect behavior!

After weeping through a box of tissues, I was done purging. All the poison infiltrating my being was released. It was my first therapy session and although it was emotionally grueling, it was also enlightening. I learned that since I was a minor and wasn't being *physically* abused, the counselor realistically couldn't do anything to change my situation. I was a child and as such, I really didn't have a voice. But the counselor's compassion and understanding helped me get through that difficult year.

When spring came that year, Jennifer gave me a little green postcard with a sticker of a little girl on one side and a flower on the other side. The card simply said, in her handwriting:

"All my life I will remember you. You brought happiness to my life, seriousness, and made me grateful for life in general. A true friend is always alive and always a friend and you will forever be remembered, *even if circumstances do not permit meetings*. In my memory you shall forever live as a beautiful, warm, loving person that sparkles with energy, beauty, wit and love. Keep your head up. Don't feel sorry for yourself. You will always have love, and I love you. Strength...Love, Jennifer."

Sadly, Jennifer moved away. She attended another school the following year, and we lost touch. I still wonder what she's doing today and whether she realizes how much her support meant.

From the age of ten until I reached eighteen, writing became the crutch that supported my broken JW adolescence, but even journaling wasn't enough to hold me up. My fragile emotional state was splintering the crutch with each passing day. To cope, I stuffed some of my negative feelings into food. Night after night, my mother would make a huge dinner and, at her beckoning, I'd usually have seconds. About an hour later I'd make a large pepperoni pizza with extra cheese and eat the whole thing. If we didn't have pizza, I found pleasure by filling a tray full of ice cream, potato chips, beef jerky, candy and other junk food. It was a personal goal to see how much food I could consume in one sitting before bedtime. I began living for food and as soon as I finished one meal, I started thinking about the next.

Both my mother and father consumed food until they were uncomfortably full, and unlimited junk food was the norm in our house. For farm people, food is love and you always "clean your plate!" I lived to go grocery shopping with my mother. It was my only recreation. The local store was about thirty minutes away, so when we ventured out into scary "worldly territory," we'd purchase large quantities of food. My overindulgence became so self-abusive that mother punished me. Even that didn't deter me. Then one day my brother's cruel, but brutally honest remarks gave me pause. (Brothers can always be counted on to tell you the truth.) He likened me to a pig and delivered a fairly realistic "oinking" sound. I was furious at him, of course, but his insight caused me to take a serious look at myself. Had he not displayed his typical obnoxious behavior, I'm sure I'd be a seriously overweight food addict today. At the time, I didn't understand why I abused food, but nowadays we better understand the term "eating disorder." Losing control in my life was making me emotionally and physically ill. Fortunately, I was able to recognize and control this disorder in its earliest stages, before it controlled me. Today I see food simply as nourishment; I no longer use it to anaesthetize pain. Although I must admit that raspberries still soothe my soul!

My external, suffocating, gray reality had nearly drained my will to live during my preteen years. Many times I felt like I was being swept under the emotional torrents. However, still waters were right around the bend in the form of an Earthly guardian angel, a caring relative who literally stepped in, plucked me from the current and saved my life.

Chapter 5: The Cocoon Weakens

> *Too often we underestimate the power of a touch, a smile, a kind word, a listening ear, an honest compliment, or the smallest act of caring, all of which have the potential to turn a life around.*
>
> Leo Buscaglia

When I was thirteen, a relative came into my life, perceptive enough to see my anger and depression, even though my family wore blinders. One spring day my mother's only living sister visited from Colorado. When she arrived, my mother offered my aunt her bed (in our room). That first night, the conversations I had with my aunt changed my life, giving me **hope** and fortifying my **dreams**. Our conversation was the prelude to a chain of events that later led to the unraveling of the Jehovah Witnesses' hold over me, a process that eventually liberated me.

I always admired my aunt. She was a successful businesswoman, financially secure, worldly and optimistic. She was very kind to our whole family (even my mother who, needless to say, repeatedly tried to convert her). As one of eleven children born into poverty, she had educated herself and excelled as a Realtor beyond everyone's expectations. She was my role model. During my preteen years, she always sent me some money tucked lovingly inside a birthday card. Of course, my mother wouldn't allow me to accept her gift. I appreciated my aunt for reaching out to me, and I resented my mother for taking away her love and those highly desired greenbacks.

Still, I vividly **dreamed** of moving to Colorado and starting a new life. After about six months as a Jehovah's Witness, I realized that even if I never had an opportunity to move to Colorado, somehow I had to create a *normal* life again. I refused to be a poor farmer's wife, have a bunch of kids, religiously attend meetings at the Kingdom Hall and beat my children into submission on that anthill. I deserved more than that and so did my future offspring.

As controlling as my mother had become, I was surprised when she let my aunt sleep in the same room with me. Obviously she underestimated us. Before we drifted off to sleep that night, my aunt asked me how I felt about the Jehovah's Witnesses. At first I was very hesitant to be honest with her. I secretly wondered if she was a spy sent by my mother. (JWs are groomed for paranoia.) But honestly, I didn't care if she was. I was bursting to confide in *someone* how I really felt—that I actually despised how the religion controlled every aspect of my life. I relayed how unhappy I was—unhappy to the point of being suicidal—and that I didn't know what to do. I started to cry. She took me in her arms and whispered that I needed to focus on getting my education and persevere. She asked me to never hurt myself but to keep praying for deliverance. She never laid out a plan for my life that night, but I knew in my heart that she loved me, supported me, and would ultimately be the catalyst that would help me free myself.

My aunt and I agreed to keep in touch after she left. She provided an enormous amount of encouragement that carried me through the darkest of hours. At one point, however, my mother found out we were writing and forbade any more contact. That didn't deter me. Using my friend, Donna, as an intermediary, we continued our secret exchange. Donna mailed my letters and when my aunt answered, she mailed her letters to Donna, who then delivered my aunt's letters to me at school. Our underground network continued for years undetected.

In the ninth grade, I realized that if I remained in Pennsylvania, there was only one way I'd find a decent job (making more than minimum wage). I'd have to work in Pittsburgh like my father had done for thirty years. (Granted, prostitution was an option too, but I didn't consider it.) Anyone who lives in a small farming town knows that you go where the good jobs are—the big city. For years I watched my dad come home frustrated and exhausted from his long commute. For three hours every day he battled snowstorms, traffic, road closures and potholes that swallowed your car whole. Even then, after thirty years with the same company, he earned just enough to support his family. My mother operated on such a tight budget that I remember nearly every grocery shopping trip becoming a battle between my mother and father. I knew I had to get out of Pennsylvania.

My aunt and I seemed to share the same **hopes** for my future, but we never dared to speak them aloud. Finally, one day, I came right out and asked her in a letter if I could move to Colorado and live with her when I graduated. For a week I nervously anticipated her response. Her response devastated me: "I'd love to have you move in with us, but my husband won't agree to that," she said. My aunt admitted that my uncle was fearful that I might turn into a wild, rebellious teenager, dabbling in drugs and alcohol once I escaped from the JW zoo. I resented my uncle's premature judgment. After all, he had never met me! How could he make such assumptions? The only things I had left to hang onto—my

hopes and dreams—seemed to be snatched away. (Never steal someone's hopes and dreams for it may be all they have left.) I thought perhaps I should just give up. However, I continued writing to my aunt, hoping to convince her that she held the power in her hands to change my life.

She finally agreed but had several conditions. The first was that I get an apartment in Pennsylvania for the summer to show my parents that it was my choice to move out. She feared that if I moved to Colorado immediately upon graduation, my mother would accuse her of helping me leave and a family feud would ensue. Clearly my aunt wanted to maintain a viable relationship with her only living sister. To put her mind at ease, I assured her that I would get an apartment and start saving money for a one-way plane ticket. (Let's see...how many ten-cent magazines is that?)

The second condition was that I live in Denver with my cousin Jenelle (my aunt's daughter), and her husband Ben. In exchange for free room and board, I'd cook, clean and run errands.

The last condition was that I go to business school. The local bus system would provide my transportation. In less than a year, I'd graduate with marketable secretarial skills, find a decent job and lease my own apartment.

Perfect, right? Wrong! This wasn't exactly my **dream**. I really wanted to live with my aunt in Colorado Springs. For one thing, I felt I really needed the emotional support to survive the backlash from my parents after I left. Secondly, because my mother had cut all ties with her family when I was nine (except, of course, to preach to them), I didn't know anything about my cousin and her husband. I had never even met them! The thought of moving to a strange state and staying with strangers, albeit relatives, was very frightening to me. In all my years in Pennsylvania, I'd never ventured more than twenty miles from home. Lastly, the thought of taking a public bus on my own was absolutely terrifying.

Conversely, *my* **dream** went something like this: Move to Colorado, live with my aunt and her husband, work in a restaurant, save money for about a year, and then move to California where I'd become a rich and famous actress.

My aunt, however, insisted that I get a traditional education. She stressed that even if I got married someday and my husband financially supported us, what would I do if he died? Who would take care of me? She made me think seriously about my future and the economic risk my sister had assumed as a stay-at-home mom, never gaining any secular skills. I realize now that I was very wise to follow her advice and get an education. Living in a different city and state with strangers soon became the octane I needed to rapidly mature and propel my life forward. Seeing no better way to rid myself of my miserable existence, I reluctantly agreed.

While the oppression at home continued, in high school my spirits soared. I signed up for a creative writing class and became the editor and co-author of a book of short stories and poems. I was excited and honored to participate in my first school activity. My diary and my poetry continued to be the bellhops for the emotional baggage I carried. Every time I wrote, I checked in some of the baggage and my load became a little more bearable, at least for a while.

Although I wasn't allowed to date, my hormones were raging and I certainly noticed the opposite sex, especially Randy, a boy in my sister's congregation who made my heart flutter. Our relationship was completely platonic—we never actually went out on a date—but my mother allowed us to write to each other. (Jehovah's Witnesses believe you shouldn't date until you are old enough to be married.)

I was sure he was very interested in me. For a while I even toyed with the idea of staying in Pennsylvania just so I could someday date him. Like me, he seemed very unhappy but unlike me, he was also quite critical of himself. He also didn't seem to be a devoted Jehovah's Witness because he'd frequently miss meetings. (Even if I had a high fever and was on death's doorstep, my mother never let me miss a meeting.) I fantasized that Randy and I could eventually leave the faith together, get married and live happily ever after, just like my Ken and Barbie dolls. How fortunate for me when, a few months later, he showed up at a religious assembly with another girl on his arm. I see this as a positive event because although I felt crushed, I soon realized that my immature infatuation with him almost caused me to detour from the path I needed to take to secure my future.

Despite all the restrictions in my life, I found moments to create my own happiness and marvel at the world around me. My adoration for nature mushroomed with each passing year, and I began to experience a spiritual enlightenment that the Jehovah's Witnesses could not impose upon me. In the warmth of the sun, I felt energized and alive. While laying underneath a tree in the yard one summer day, the prickly grass poking through the cotton blanket and itching the soles of my bare feet, I watched the clouds wistfully float by and change form. It was at that moment that I realized nothing in life is really constant but change. And my life too would someday change.

With each changing season, I celebrated my life knowing I was one year, one day, closer to freedom. I remembered my grandmother's joyful singing. Despite being a poor farmer's wife, raising eleven children with a much older, sometimes-abusive man, she always managed to smile. Knowing her background helped me focus on the good things in my life and remain optimistic.

Much of my joy came from knowing a boy named Alex. He was a sophomore and I was a junior when we first laid eyes on each other. Alex was a vision, a football player with a stocky build and soft, straight, flowing blonde hair with dark highlights and mesmerizing blue eyes. Randy, my former crush, paled in comparison.

Alex had a twin brother and while his brother seemed a little arrogant, Alex appealed to me because he was soft-spoken and demure. His gentleness combined with his muscular stance drew me unavoidably in. I wondered how his firm chest would feel pressed against mine if he were to kiss me, how his breath might feel tickling the hairs of my neck, how his hands might feel touching my face.

I invented the word "stalking" before it became the buzzword to define an obsessed lover. I'd go out of my way to run into Alex every day after class, even if it meant leaving class a little early so I could race down two flights of stairs and sprint across the building. Most days I was brazen, walking directly towards him; sometimes I shyly peeked around the corner. Glee filled my heart as he approached from the opposite end of the hall. Unfortunately, sometimes I only got a brief glance at him as we passed each other, but whatever he was doing at that moment—ruffling his hair or talking to a friend or occasionally smiling back at me—that moment was etched into my memory for the next few hours, to be replayed time and again. If we ran into each other unexpectedly, I'd quickly pull my friends aside and yo-yo up and down, shrieking once he was out of sight. I was definitely infatuated!

The female species has, throughout time, been labeled as the mistresses of manipulation, and I was no exception. Alex's house was the last stop before school and by the time he and his brother got on, there were usually only one or two seats available. So every morning, I'd grab an empty seat, then drape my legs across the seat so that no one else would want to sit with me. As I watched the bus fill to capacity around me, I knew if I kept my seat open, Alex (or, regrettably, his brother!) would eventually be forced to sit with me.

Whenever the bus hit a bump in the road, we sometimes rubbed shoulders. (Thank God for potholes! With each jostle, I was definitely one of those rare Jehovah's Witnesses—one of 144,000—who had made it to heaven!) If the bus took a sharp turn, our knees would touch and my heart would skip a beat. Even so, I was too nervous to really converse with him. Our limited conversations, "Hi, how are you?" followed by "Fine!" continued for the next two years.

Following my graduation, Alex finally made a move to get a little closer. But before I tell you about that one summer day with Alex, I need to tell you how I broke out of the cocoon that encapsulated me.

Chapter 6: Breaking Free

> *Not everything that is faced can be changed, but nothing can be changed until it is faced.*
>
> James A. Baldwin

During my senior year, I impatiently counted down the days and hours until the end of my prison sentence. I knew plans for my deliverance from the Jehovah's Witnesses had to be sketched quickly. First and foremost, I had to earn enough money to get myself to Colorado. And with a plane ticket costing several hundred dollars, that wasn't going to be easy!

Fortunately, a golden opportunity emerged for me to earn money in my junior year. My school was having a candy fundraiser to pay for the senior class prom later in the year. The winner would receive $125. Now, to the average person, $125 doesn't seem like enough money to alter a person's life, but I just knew that with that much money in my pocket, the world was about to become my oyster, or at least I might have a chance to find a pearl in it. I pleaded with my mother to allow me to participate. Much to my amazement, she agreed. (Hey, that's *one* thing the Jehovah's Witnesses don't prohibit.)

My father, however, scoffed at the idea, suggesting it was a scam: "I doubt the school will cough up a penny," he cautioned. That's my father—always the skeptic. (This attribute saved him from being baptized years earlier.) I argued vehemently until Dad conceded. He said he'd eat his words if he found a check from the school sitting on his dinner plate. I set out on a mission: to prove him wrong.

This was probably the first and only time in my life that being a Jehovah's Witness paid off for me. Because I had gone door-to-door preaching for so many years, I was now fairly confident about approaching strangers. Besides, I was peddling delectable candy this time, not cramming religion down people's throats (big difference).

So every day after school, I'd gather as many $1 candy bars and $2 boxes of candy that I could carry onto the bus. My classmates usually helped me load up the bus seats around me. When the bus pulled up to my house, I'd lug the boxes off, carefully constructing a cardboard chain at the bottom of our driveway. Then, one by one, I'd load the boxes into my parent's car until there was little room for anything else, save me in the driver's seat. Every evening for two weeks, I'd descend upon highly populated areas, utilizing my charms and exuberant smile to make a sale. I never went home until I sold out. I didn't know if I was in first place or not, but I knew I had to give it everything I had if I wanted to ensure success. For me, this wasn't about selling candy but rather, buying freedom.

When the sales were tallied and the results conveyed to the class, I was stunned. I had broken the previous year's record by $300 and had sold $640 worth of candy. I hadn't just won first place—I left the second place winner in the dust! Later that month, in a fleeting moment of fame, my name appeared in the local newspaper. Success never tasted so sweet![5]

When my father came home that evening, he found a $125 check neatly situated on his plate and an ear-to-ear grin on my face. He picked it up, looked at me and chuckled. For the first time, my father saw how much determination his usually passive daughter could muster. (It certainly wasn't the last time he'd see it.) I spent about $40 of the $125 on two practical items: a black beanbag chair and a rose-etched table lamp that I had coveted months earlier. (I knew I'd need some light when I moved into an apartment after graduation and *something* to sit on.) I pocketed the rest of the money for future necessities.

Either Jehovah was smiling down on me or I was *finally* getting a well-deserved break. I wasn't sure which force was at work in my life, but in my senior year I learned that there is always a rainbow on the horizon—if you just ride out the storm and keep your eyes wide open.

A few weeks later another fantastic opportunity arose for me to earn even *more* money. My school had begun a youth training program, funded through the local county's Employment and Training Administration, offering plumbing, home furnishings, electronics and photography classes. If selected, I'd be able to earn minimum wage (about $3 an hour) and learn a new skill. I approached Mother with the premise that if I earned extra money I could begin buying my own clothes after graduation. I knew she'd see this as a downright advantageous proposition. After all, for years she had purchased clothing for three kids on an extremely tight budget. Of course, I never told her that my best friend, Cindy, was also interested in the

---

[5] Ironically, when I became a senior the following year, I wasn't permitted to attend my own senior prom, in spite of the fact that I had raised the most money the previous year for the junior prom. What a disappointment!

program or that I really wanted the money to escape from
the clutches of her religious cult.

Cindy and I applied for the photography and home
furnishings classes. Well, someone on the deciding
committee obviously had a peculiar sense of humor because
we wound up in the *plumbing* class. We weren't too thrilled
and assumed we'd be the only girls in an *all-boy* class. To the
contrary, we were assigned to an *all-girl* plumbing outfit. We
truly questioned the sensibility of it. Girls learning
plumbing? Why on Earth would they want to? Visions of
clearing nasty, stinky toilets clogged with poop and toilet
paper danced in our heads. Any support we may have had for
feminism at that moment was usurped by the notion that we
were hurling women—*us*—back to the dark ages. But it was
money. And just like our junior high school that initially
seemed so dreary and awful, I learned quickly that
appearances can be deceiving. Tackling a male-dominated
profession turned out to be one of the highlights of my
senior year!

Our plumbing teacher—Mr. D, as we fondly referred to
him—was only about 5'4", incredibly shy, and as adorable as
a teddy bear. We loved to tease him and make him laugh with
our antics and flirtatious jokes. People frequently asked him
how it felt to be outnumbered with all those girls in his class.
He would just shake his head and smile. We knew he loved
every delicious moment of it.

During the next five months, we built a powder room
from scratch using two-by-four lumber. Once the framework
was done, we installed a floor, sink, water closet (and
fortunately it had no nasty clogs) and copper pipes. We
became known as the "Plumberettes," monikers that
appeared on the back of our own "official" shirts. We even
managed to get our picture published in the local paper. Once
again, I was a local celebrity. After taxes, I had earned about
$200, which I put into my "flight for freedom" fund.

I wasn't sure if my mother had temporarily lost her mind or if "the other God" (i.e., not the Jehovah's Witnesses gloom-and-doom God) finally answered *my* prayers, but I was finally getting a taste of independence, of that sweet freedom that so many of my peers took for granted. Because mother permitted me to drive the family car to school during my work program, I took some liberties, as most teenagers would do—liberties that my parents never knew about. In fact, I did the unthinkable. Yes, I indulged in every parent's worst nightmare, every parent's worst fear. OK, maybe not every parent's—just *my* parent's fear. I confess. I...I...took several friends to a restaurant during our lunch break and...and we had sandwiches! *That's it.* My sin? I associated with "worldly" people. At the not-so-tender age of eighteen, I finally got to see—for the first time—what it felt like to hang out with friends! But that was just the beginning...

On the way to school one morning, I detoured to pick up Cindy. We had planned to drive down Alex's dirt road just before the bus came so we could watch him strut his stuff to the bus stop from a safe, obscure distance. But wouldn't you know it, he spotted us! Now, imagine our reaction. Here we are, two teenage girls with hormones in overdrive and a hunky football player approaching the car. Our reaction was equivalent to two hummingbirds being overdosed on sugar water. Cindy, being the good friend she was, always became as exuberant as I, both of us squealing at each other with wide eyes and Cheshire Cat grins. "Oh, my God! Ohhhh, my God! Here he comes! What should we do?"

Alex meandered over to my car window with a puzzled look. He leaned down so he could poke his head through my open window and flatly announced, "Hi!" with a big smile on his face. I gave him some courteous reply, concealing my excitement, and then inquired if he wanted a ride. Hey, I had to come up with something fast, and saying, "Ahhhhh, I just drove in here to stare at your delectable, perfect body," didn't seem quite appropriate. He said he would need to check with his dad first and asked if I could pick him up the next day instead. I agreed, praying all the while that my mother wouldn't hear about the lunch date or our detour and revoke my driving privileges. As I said good-bye, I desperately tried to refrain from squealing like that sow I used to wrestle. Eureka!

But, alas, there was a problem. The road to Alex's house was only one lane, so I could not simply turn around. I thought, "No problem. I'll just back the car out." I discovered immediately how much Alex's presence—just seeing his divine face—had rattled me. My frazzled condition sent my nervous system into spasms. As I backed up, I punched the accelerator and the car rolled up over the embankment and nearly flipped over before we came down the other side. Can you imagine my embarrassment? Alex just smiled and shook his finger at me. I thought, "Oh great. He'll never ride with us now." But I was wrong. The next day, I drove all of us to school, on Clouds Nine, Ten, and Eleven the whole way.

Toward the end of my senior year, my parents offered to host a graduation party for me. I was genuinely surprised and elated. How thoughtful! My mother *was* really coming around. There appeared to be some **hope** for our relationship. Perhaps I wouldn't need to leave home after all. Perhaps I had misjudged my mother. Perhaps now that I was older, she was willing to bend the Jehovah's Witnesses' rules a bit so I could lead a more normal life. Perhaps she could see how I was emotionally distancing myself from her, and she was trying to extend the ladder to reach me. Perhaps. Perhaps not.

I innocently asked my mother how many friends I could invite. She paused, wrinkled her eyebrows and coolly remarked, "Oh, no. You can't invite anyone from school— only Jehovah's Witnesses!" Was she saying what I thought she was saying? Yes, I could have a graduation party, but I couldn't even invite *one* of my friends? The only people at the party would be 50ish, married JW couples with whom I had nothing in common. I truly didn't even care to be in the same room with these people! Was my life this surreal?

Seeing the pain in my tearing eyes, my father spoke up on my behalf for the very first time. He begged my mother to compromise, to let just one friend attend, but she held firm—no outsiders. She definitely ruled the roost.

Although I could feel myself becoming enraged, I didn't let her restrictions dash any opportunities coming my way. Instead, I reasoned that these Witnesses might give me enough moola to afford the price of freedom. As much as I had craved the opportunity to forge friendships during the last nine years, I craved my freedom a thousand times more. I reluctantly agreed to her terms—a graduation with no friends.

I didn't realize it at the time, but the Witnesses were teaching me that *acceptance* of any situation (outside of my control) could be liberating, if I applied the right filters. Like a butterfly, I was experiencing a metamorphosis within this cocoon.

That same year my brother, who was now twenty-eight, proposed to his girlfriend Meg, whom he had been dating for almost a year. Meg and I always got along well, even though, quite frankly, I had no idea what she saw in my brother. While most siblings argue a lot when they are living under the same roof as children, I always knew that my brother and I would never be close. He was unusually immature well into his late twenties, always jumping through the air, pretending to fly and spouting, "I'm Captain America" or some other hero jargon. As the tattletale of the family, he really irritated me—always trying to get me into trouble with my mother when I failed to study JW literature. And I could go on and on about how lazy he was, but part of that was the family culture I grew up in. "Bro" was antisocial as well, always burying himself in his room, listening to one of his one thousand record albums. My parents enabled his irresponsible behavior by allowing him to spend all of the money he earned on music. Looking back, I think he used music to soothe his soul like I used poetry, but unlike me, he never had the courage to become a dissenter.

My brother only had one dispute with my mother that I can remember. He wanted to let his hair grow past the tops of his ears but my mother emphatically denied his request. All male Jehovah's Witnesses are forbidden to have long hair and/or beards, which is curious given that men in Biblical times, even Jesus, supposedly had beards and long hair. I don't remember him giving her much of a fight about it, although he certainly could've stood firm—he was in his early twenties after all. But I think staying in my mother's good graces was more important to my brother than anything. As her firstborn and only son, he knew he was her favorite. He became the epitome of an obedient Jehovah's Witness and eventually he too was made an Elder.

When Meg asked me to be a bridesmaid at her wedding, I felt compelled to oblige. Although I felt guilty (I knew I would be leaving her beloved religion soon), I also felt honored to participate because my own sister's decision to *not* include me, her only sister, in her wedding years earlier had left me feeling unappreciated. My brother and Meg were married at the Kingdom Hall in May 1980. I was hopeful for my brother because he was finally able to leave home, right? Well, not really. He and his new wife moved into an old mobile home on my parents' property—just a few yards from their farmhouse. That's not exactly what I would call cutting (or even stretching) the umbilical cord. But I guess it was a baby step to independence.

Toward the end of my senior year, I finally began to rebel. I don't really like to use that word because I don't consider myself a rebel at all. When I think of the word "rebel," I think of someone who defies authority and order to their own detriment. That wasn't me. I still had the values my parents had instilled in me. I didn't smoke, drink alcohol, have sex (didn't even date) or swear. I was the model child. When I took a stance, it was because at this time in my life I realized that there was little else my mother (or anyone else) could do to hurt me. Reminiscent of a terminally ill woman who decides for the first time in her life to parachute out of a plane because she wants to feel the wind in her face as she free-falls, I knew I had nothing left to lose—even if my parachute failed to open. After all, the life I had been living was a far cry from living.

With all the courage I could muster, I matter-of-factly informed my mother that I was going to my senior class banquet that evening. Because I hadn't been asked to my senior prom earlier that year (I would have been viewed more datable had I been a witch instead of a Witness)—nor was I permitted to go—I knew this was my last opportunity to participate in a real school function. Well, her predictable response was, "You will not!" To which I replied emphatically, "Oh, yes, I will!" I think my recalcitrant behavior shocked my mother for she stopped and looked utterly dismayed. I had outright defied her! When those words came out of my mouth, even I didn't recognize the person speaking.

Although quaking like a seedling trying to stand firm in the face of a tornado, I went upstairs and managed to get ready, with Mother quoting a monologue of scriptures the whole time. I turned a deaf ear and tried to block out the guilt that consumed me for disobeying her.

Thirty minutes later, one of my friends picked me up and away we went. It was a marvelous dinner. There was so much activity, so much enchantment. I absorbed everything: the floral decorations on the tables, the marvelous taste of the Italian food, the incessant chatter and laughter in the room, even the eccentric hypnotist who provided our entertainment. I felt like Cinderella escaping from the evil stepmother.

This is where the story gets a little fuzzy due to the extreme emotional energy being expended (i.e., all the screaming going back and forth). When I got home that night, I do remember locking the bedroom door and shortly thereafter my father threatening to kick it in. And I remember yelling, "I don't give a *#@!" to my mother as she was trying to preach to me through the closed door. This was also the first time I ever swore at my parents. My dad intervened and I agreed to open the door and talk to him— alone. Mother conceded and left the room as my father and I had our first "Come to Jesus Meeting." I told him I hated the religion, I had no intention of staying in it, and that my teen years had been Hell. During my unforeseen breakdown, I also told him that if I couldn't invite my own friends to *my* graduation party, I didn't want their stupid party. (Not one of my better moves. So much for the moola.)

My father tried to get us to calm down and go to sleep because, as he pointed out, "It's late and I have to get up for work at 4 a.m.!" In many ways, I don't think he realized how unwavering I could be because up until then I had been the perfect, obedient daughter. He probably thought I was just having a severe case of PMS (premenstrual syndrome) and would simply get over it. (My father remained in this state of denial for many, many years.)

As Mother and I lay in our beds within inches of each other, she continued to preach to me, firing off the appropriate scriptures, all the while trying to suppress her obvious anger. After about fifteen minutes of her relentless badgering, I threatened to leave if she didn't stop. Of course, I didn't have the faintest idea where I would go in the dark, out in the boonies, but she could tell I meant it. She hesitantly stopped talking for a few minutes. Being the unbridled fanatic that she was, she couldn't resist quoting one more scripture, to which I countered: "AH, AH, AH, if you start preaching, you just lied to me, and that's a S...I...N!" For once, I used my knowledge about her religion to assault her right back. With that, the preaching finally ceased. Feeling marvelously empowered—and with my blood pressure returning to normal—I slowly drifted off to sleep. I tried to block out her prayers from the next bed: "Jehovah, please guide Brenda back to you. Help her to resist Satan. Give her the wisdom..."

The next day at breakfast she took up right where she had left off the night before. "I'm calling an Elder," she announced. Well, I had had more than enough. There was absolutely no way I was going to have any more grueling brainwashing sessions with the Elders, who seemed to thrive on "providing loving assistance." I decided to write a note and leave it on the couch. It simply said, "I went to talk to the trees. At least they will listen to me!" (That was my way of letting her know I had not been kidnapped but was just taking a walk in the woods. Being the conscientious daughter that I was, it was not my intention to unduly alarm her.) I then tiptoed down the steps and slinked out the basement door. Beyond the long, open stretch of road stood a grove of trees about three-quarters of a mile from our house. If I reached the edge of it, I could disappear into the woods and she wouldn't see me when she came looking for me. I knew I had about five to ten minutes before she found the note, so I really hauled butt. However, I was so consumed with anguish it felt as though I was dragging dead weight with every step. Would I be able to make it into the safety of the trees before she found me? Every moment that passed felt like a slow-motion dream. With every tear that fell from my face, I felt like my heart was going to implode. Would I be able to stop crying long enough to see my way clearly? Would I be able to live just one moment of peace? Couldn't she see that she wasn't just throwing me under the bus; she was telling the driver to put it into reverse, to back over me once more in order to leave a deeper impression? Was preaching scripture day in and day out all she cared about? Didn't she care enough about me to help me survive *this* world? Forget the "New Order." I needed to survive **now**!

Not a moment too soon I skirted under the barbed-wire fence that surrounded the pasture leading to the forest. I had barely reached the outskirts of the trees when I spotted mother driving up the road toward me. "B..r..e..n..d..a! B..r..e..n..d..a!" she yelled repeatedly, stretching my name into infinity. I lunged behind a big oak tree and stayed low until she drove on by. She never spotted me. After she passed, I shouted with delight, "Hallelujah!" (which, according to the JWs, means "Praise Jehovah!")

Although my best friend Cindy's house was less than two miles away, it was the first time in my entire life that I had ever walked there. She greeted me with a perplexed look and then noticed I'd been crying. Lovingly, she put her arm around my shoulders and guided me inside her home. We sat at her old wooden kitchen table and talked to her mom about my struggles, about how I was afraid to go back home, about how I was terrified something awful might happen. Here I was at a critical breaking point and facing a crossroads in my life.

Later that day, Cindy and I telephoned our classmate, Lane, and together we drove back to my house. (Yes, there is safety in numbers, or at least a sense of safety.) Once inside, we haphazardly swept all my belongings (i.e., my clothes, beanbag chair, and lamp) into Lane's car. When my mother saw what I was doing, she became hysterical. At this point, however, I had little compassion toward her. The feelings I had for my cat when he swatted those baby birds from the nest and injured them swelled to the surface. Deep down I loved her, but I also really hated her. I knew that losing her last two children from the "nest" in the same month would tear her apart, and I felt guilty. However, any qualms I may have had about hurting her took a back seat to my survival. I was now the baby bird thrown from the nest, and I had to live to tell the tale of what I had endured. She had no idea what she had subjected me to—and never would.

As we started to drive away, my mother reached through my open car window and tightly squeezed my neck, sobbing uncontrollably. She only released her grip once the car's acceleration ripped me from her grasp, but even then she continued to run beside the car. When she could no longer keep up, she stopped and threw her tear-soaked face into the palms of her hands. I knew I was responsible for her wrenching grief. In her mind, it was as though I had just died, or at least just condemned myself to death. (The only other time I had seen my mother cry profusely was a night many, many years earlier when she learned her brother had been killed by a burglar.) While I felt empathy for her and fought back the sick, sinking feeling that encompassed my heart, I also felt strangely liberated. Like a deer caught in headlights, the brilliant light of her religion had controlled and paralyzed me. Which way should I run? How will I see my escape route if I am blinded by the spotlight on me? And like a deer, it was my agile, free spirit that dodged those lights and took that leap of faith to reach the banks of safety.

For the first time in nearly a decade, since she answered that door and talked to that "nice" Elder, Mother realized she could not tell me how to live my life. I was eighteen years old and my life belonged to *me*. Legally, there was nothing she could do to force me to come home. I knew that—and she knew that. In that brief, unsullied moment, she must have felt utterly helpless, as helpless as she had made me feel for the last nine years.

Cindy's home became my home, my oasis in the desert, for the next few weeks until we graduated. I will forever be grateful to her mother for having the courage and compassion to become involved in my moment of crisis. What a brave and generous woman!

I have an old plaque in my bedroom that sits on my headboard. It simply says: "There is only one success...to be able to live your life in your own way." It's a motto I have lived by every day since. And it's the only way to *live*!

The last few weeks of school hurried by, and I knew I couldn't live with Cindy and her folks forever. I filled out job applications for nineteen different restaurants. In the poor economy of that farming area, only one fast food company (Wendy's) even called me back. I was thrilled when they hired me on the spot during the interview. At least now I could support myself. Or could I?

Lane and I barely knew each other but decided to become roommates to economize. We scoured the newspaper ads and found a newly constructed, one-bedroom duplex to lease in a nearby town. Our plan was to move in on June 1 and by mid-July Karla, Lane's best friend, would join us from Oregon. The three of us would split all expenses, including rent, which was less than $200 per month. I had waited patiently for independence—nearly a decade. And very soon, in what would now feel like the blink of an eye, the missing pieces of my life would be reassembled into a colorful puzzle.

My senior year had come and gone. Although my parents attended the ceremony, we really didn't know what to say to each other. My graduation was yet another bittersweet milestone in my childhood.

As for the graduation party, it never materialized. Not one JW even sent me a card. Talk about conditional love! How can the followers of any religion—especially a religion that professes to be worshipping a God of love—so abruptly discard someone they have known for nearly a decade? Even my father, who rarely said anything negative about the Witnesses, remarked that he thought it was terrible that the Elder who came to our door that fateful summer day—the very same Elder who had watched me grow up, who had befriended my family—would now eschew me. I went from being called "Freckles" and "Brenda the beloved" to being branded a "goat," a "nonbeliever," and a "lost soul" manipulated by Satan. My mother stood by and watched me endure their emotional abuse, much like she tolerated the physical abuse bestowed by my teacher years earlier. What's worse, she wasn't simply a willing bystander; she was about to become an active participant in shunning her own daughter.

If I had had even the slightest doubt about what I was leaving behind, it quickly vanished when the entire congregation discarded me. The Jehovah's Witnesses quote this gem from the scriptures and believe it applies only to them: "You shall know The Truth and The Truth shall set you free." Little did they know that I had seen The Truth about them, and yes, it set me free!

Chapter 7: Prostitution and Thievery

Wealth is in the richness of the mind and heart, not the pocket.

Anay Bathia

To suggest that Lane and I moved into our duplex with ample possessions would be like referring to the climb up Mount Everest as merely a "little jaunt." Between the two of us, we had one cooking skillet, one beanbag chair, one lamp, a few rusty kitchen utensils and a thirteen-inch portable TV (with lousy reception, I might add). I didn't even have a bed to sleep on because my mother couldn't find it in her heart to relinquish my bed when I moved out. For a while I slept on the floor until my devoted grandmother took pity on me and gave me an old roll-up cot to use. It had a lumpy, stained mattress and a protruding jagged metal frame (which one day gave me a large gash in my leg), but it was very welcome nonetheless. Lane set up two single beds next to my cot—one for her and one for Karla. All three beds were sandwiched together in our tiny bedroom, much like the dwarfs' accommodations in Walt Disney's *Snow White and the Seven Dwarfs*. (At least I wasn't shacking up with seven men!)

Grandma surprised me with a hand-sewn quilt so I'd have something warm to snuggle into. That single gesture meant so much more to me than the tidbits of cloth and thread used to bind it together. For me, that blanket was a symbol of the comfort and acceptance that my grandmother was willing to share, even though she knew her daughter, my mother, wasn't willing to offer the same. I imagined her hands, wrinkled, unsteady and tired from years of responsibilities, carefully stitching each square in place hour after hour. I imagined that she wept inside over the struggles I'd endured with my mother. She probably wondered, as I had, why mother had denied us our visits over the last decade. Oh, how I adored my grandma and relished the opportunity to spend precious time with her again.

Despite having practically nothing, I felt like I had everything. It reminded me of the movie *St. Elmo's Fire*. In one scene, Wendy (played by the actress, Mare Winningham) describes her life after moving into her first apartment. She recounts waking in the middle of the night to make a P&J (peanut butter and jelly) sandwich. As she sat alone in her kitchen she marveled at how it was the best PB&J sandwich she had ever eaten—because she was in her *own* place. I knew exactly what she was feeling in that scene. For the first time in many, many years, I had my grandma, my friends, my freedom, holidays to celebrate and Saturday morning cartoons!

Although June was our first month of independence and incredibly thrilling, July and August were admittedly difficult. The hours for my fast-food job were drastically cut to ten hours per week. At $3 per hour minimum wage, I was barely making enough money (after taxes) to cover my share of the $200 rent. Instead, I was treading financial quicksand and sinking rapidly. Lane was not working at all because she felt it was beneath her to work a fast-food job. She opted to hold out for a potential opening at a local automotive factory that paid a whopping $10 per hour. I tried to persuade her to accept work anywhere, pointing out that she was an unskilled worker and therefore needed to accept an entry-level job first, but my advice fell on deaf ears.

We always met our financial obligations (such as rent and car insurance) because we did have a little savings going into this venture, but groceries eventually dwindled to just a few condiments in the fridge. Having ketchup as the main course for dinner sure didn't sound appealing. While Lane managed to scrounge food from her aunt and uncle by frequently showing up at their house right around suppertime, I couldn't count on the same from my parents. So, I survived— thank you, Wendy's!—by eating other people's discarded garbage (French fries mostly and occasionally a bite or two of a leftover hamburger). I became a closet eater in the literal sense. You see, it was my job to clear the trays and food left behind by dumping them into the trash, located in a little alcove between the dining room and kitchen. This discrete niche gave me the opportunity to gobble food down before anyone could see me. For two months, I lived on French fries. It's truly a miracle the blood in my arteries didn't coagulate into a vat of grease!

Mom and Dad seldom visited me that summer. Jehovah's Witnesses believe that if you refrain offering emotional or financial support to a person who has left The Truth, then that worldly one will possibly see the error of their ways and come back with their tail between their legs when the going gets tough.

Quite frankly, their absence from my life was a welcome reprieve. Who wouldn't prefer peace to conflict? Seeing my mother, after all, only produced anxiety and heartache for both of us. On one such routine visit I was stunned when Mother informed me that I would become a thief and prostitute now that Satan had taken hold of me. I looked at her with unqualified disbelief and pity as I picked my jaw up off the floor. How sad that she didn't even know her own daughter!

If I called my mom from the pay phone at the local bowling alley, she'd beg me to come home. She'd relay how she'd just taken some homemade beef stew or fresh apple pie to my sister. (My mother made the best desserts from the cherries, apples and raspberries she got from the farm.) Her words always invoked anger. She obviously didn't care that I was starving. Suddenly she became the person I had read about in her religious magazines as a child—the heartless sadist who rubbed salt into the wounds of those who had been beaten. But honestly, I would have lived under a bridge and eaten out of trash cans the rest of my life before I ever went "home."

Now, every child wants to please her parents, and knowing I couldn't be in my mother's good graces like my brother and sister cut me deeply. But I was also mature enough to realize that it wasn't Mother who was speaking. Any vestige of who she was—and any common sense she may have had—was annihilated when the Jehovah's Witnesses started shoveling negativity and delusions into her malleable mind.

In my eyes, my sister and brother got everything—love, financial assistance when they needed it, and most importantly, *a mother who was there for them.* I resented my siblings; and yet, even as a young child, I knew a tumultuous road lay ahead. The repercussions felt by anyone who left the Jehovah's Witnesses were always severe.

Fortunately, Karla arrived from Oregon with some money she had saved. Her finances gave us the stability we needed to continue. Alas, emotional stability for our little group would prove a little harder to come by. We learned Lane's uncle was sexually molesting her. I believe he felt entitled to repayment for providing all those "free" meals. Lane put up with it, frequently complaining about how much she hated what he was doing, but she stubbornly refused to halt visitation. I felt powerless to help her, so the best I could do was offer her a shoulder to cry on when she needed it.

After several weeks, Lane applied for welfare when she saw the automotive job wasn't going to materialize. Remarkably, even though she was eighteen and fully capable of working, the state of Pennsylvania approved her application. I found her work ethic less than honorable. The food stamps she received, however, provided a much-needed staple for all of us, and we accepted them with much gratitude. What a blessing it was to be able to go to the grocery store and have the means to purchase something besides French fries! I fondly recall that first grand shopping spree—loading up on Ho Ho's, ice cream and other junk food—things we hadn't eaten for months. Just like a typical teenager.

At times, Lane seemed downright psychotic. She'd lock Karla and me out of the apartment and become not only emotionally but also physically abusive, sometimes hitting and scratching deep enough to draw blood. Although Karla and I were initially strangers going into this venture, we ultimately became the best of friends. I believe Lane resented our blossoming friendship and, in turn, projected the anger she was feeling towards her uncle back on us. As a result, Karla didn't stay with us for very long. After numerous fights with Lane, she ended up going back to Oregon. Karla and Lane never spoke again, but Karla and I became pen pals for over a decade after she left.

My relationship with Lane (especially our financial situation) grew increasingly precarious. We knew we had to get another roommate or we'd become homeless, or worse yet—kill each other.

Lane convinced her friend and former classmate, Valerie, to move in with us. Valerie had two boyfriends (both truckers) who occasionally drove through town. When they visited, she had sex with both of them—a ménage a trois. One day Valerie told me her two male friends thought I was attractive and wondered if I'd like to have sex. While I consider myself a very liberal-minded person, I knew I'd regret it if I engaged in sex with these two men. At eighteen, I was still a virgin, and I wanted my first sexual experience to be with someone who would make it both special and memorable, someone I could feel safe with. Consequently, I declined the invitation. Little did I know that I was about to lose my virginity to someone I absolutely adored.

Maybe I am just an eternal optimist, but as I stated earlier, I believe that a brilliant rainbow has followed every dark cloud in my life. Alex was my arc of spectral colors, my vision, when he suddenly materialized in our driveway on September 6, 1980.

I had been out playing kickball in the fields with our landlord's teenage daughter and was a mess. As anyone who has visited the lusciously green state of Pennsylvania knows, the summer humidity there is unforgiving. My hair was drenched in sweat, my makeup had melted away, and I desperately needed a shower. Imagine my unequivocal disbelief, followed by simultaneous elation and horror, when Alex pulled into our driveway, stepped out of his car, and asked me out. All I could think was, "Why, of all times, do I have to look and smell like an old, wet dish towel?" I did say, "Yes—Yes—Yes!" but asked him if he wouldn't mind waiting while I took a quick shower first. I dried my hair with one hand and applied makeup with the other. In record time, I took a copper penny and turned it into a million bucks.

We went to see a movie and, quite frankly, I can't remember the title or even what it was about. (I was obviously in a state of shock.) Shortly after we took our seats,

Alex reached over and wrapped his hand around mine with an ease that indicated he had performed this maneuver before. I felt every hair on the back of his hand, every caress of his fingertips, every bit of sweat exchanged between us. And every moment that passed was surreal.

After the movie, we drove back to my duplex. I was expecting to see my roommates, but as we walked through the doorway, I realized we were alone. It was a tranquil, late summer evening with a faint chill creeping into the air, signaling autumn was right around the corner. We plopped down onto my beanbag chair. Robins serenaded us from the maple tree outside as we made awkward small talk. In a bold instant, he leaned towards me. I became acutely aware of his face inches away from mine, invading my comfort zone. I didn't pull away, even though bolts of electricity surged through our bodies. Alex began softly kissing me, pausing briefly, searching my lips for approval to continue. I remember running my hand through his silky blonde hair and saying, "I've always wanted to do that." He smiled faintly as though he secretly knew my desires. We talked and kissed some more, and then he gazed into my eyes. All of a sudden, he whispered:

"Would you like to make love?"

When he said those two little words, "make love," it felt like the wind had been knocked out of me. My sexuality was already flaming and the embarrassing dampness between my legs seemed ever so obvious. His words felt exhilarating, frightening, enticing.

I knew from talking to Alex in school earlier that year that he had a long-distance relationship with another girl, and that he planned to eventually marry her. When he showed up that day, I suspected he came to me just to have sex, and his frank inquiry confirmed my suspicions. But I really didn't care if he used me because I wanted *him* more than he wanted *sex*. Admittedly, I was terrified. I was a virgin after all. Plus, this was my *first* date with a boy! I debated for a monumental amount of time—about three seconds—then realized that if I were to ever lose my virginity to a man, I wanted it to be with Alex. Who would ever be more satisfying to me—this boy for whom I had lusted (shamelessly, I might add) all through high school?

I nervously took him by the hand and we walked to my romantic corner of the bedroom and plopped down on my enticing, lumpy, stained cot. I made some comment about not knowing what to do, as I had never been with a boy. He seemed surprised. Throwing caution to the wind and common sense out the window, we had your basic intercourse, which lasted a disappointing five minutes (actually, make that three minutes). Once he was done, it was obvious to me he was done visiting as well.

We stood in the open doorway of my duplex, me wearing nothing but a T-shirt and him a warm smile. He said he would come back to see me. I gave him a long hug, all the while imprinting the contours of his body in my mind, knowing full well that I would never see him again. Yet, for weeks when a car would pull into the complex, I anxiously ran to the window anticipating that Alex just might get out of the car. I knew deep inside, however, that he was but a small chapter in my life, and I accepted that. It's true that you never forget your first love.

Despite a lack of parental support, I didn't come to know prostitution or thievery as my mother predicted (unless you consider eating other people's garbage stealing). However, I did come to know myself a lot better that summer. And although I had survived life on my own outside the cocoon without being eaten alive, I suspected the most challenging and exciting times in my life still lay on the horizon.

Chapter 8: Leaving It All Behind

All changes, even the most longed for, have their melancholy; for what we leave behind us is a part of ourselves; we must die to one life before we can enter another.

Anatole France

Shortly after my date with Alex, I realized it was time for me to prepare for my move to Colorado. Somehow I had managed to save enough money to put a few bucks in my pocket for incidental expenses. But if I stayed in my current situation much longer, I knew I'd end up homeless. Clearly, I was not making it in Pennsylvania. A rural farm in Pennsylvania may have been a good place to raise a child, but with the economy the way it was, it was a lousy place to raise an adult.

My mother had created what she thought was a protected environment by keeping me inside a cocoon. But like a butterfly with soft wings, when I tried to fly free from my cocoon, I faltered. As that first summer on my own revealed, I was utterly unprepared to become an adult. My parents had failed to follow through on the most important obligation they had as parents. They had failed to create autonomy in me by letting me experience life—good and bad—providing guidance and emotional support when I needed it. If I were to have any chance of surviving outside that cocoon, I knew I needed to be part of a support system, and my parents just weren't capable of giving that to me. My childhood—living as a prisoner of the Jehovah's Witnesses and being locked away in solitary for nearly a decade under the pretense that "Jehovah will provide for all your needs"—although well intended, had actually crippled me.

For many reasons, I wanted to abandon Pennsylvania. For over half of my childhood, it held nothing but disappointment. Even my dreams were taken away. Remember when I said my brother moved into a mobile home on my father's property after he got married? My **dream**, as I had informed my family during my preteen years, was to live on that same piece of land. But after mother joined the Jehovah's Witnesses and my brother and his new wife moved their mobile home into *my* spot, my **dream** was stolen.

As the youngest in the family, I felt like I got the leftovers of everything. For years I wore my brother's and sister's hand-me-down clothing. I had to share a bedroom with my sister, and then when she moved out, I had to share it with my mother. I rode my brother's bike and racked myself on the bar when I tried to dismount. (I never understood what useful purpose that horizontal bar served.) At the same time, because I *was* the youngest, I knew my father adored me. Although my brother and sister physically resembled him, I clearly had his spirit and savvy, which I think he admired and respected.

Finding the courage to tell my dad that I was leaving was one of the hardest things I have ever done, because I knew it would absolutely devastate him. I recalled my father's uneasiness when my sister got married to a Jehovah's Witness and moved sixty miles away. He accepted the inevitable but found it hard to let go emotionally. He always wanted his children to live within arm's reach. How would he cope when I moved one thousand miles away?

I was looking for courage to convey my **hopes** and **dreams** but was at a loss for words. My dad always loved the Wizard of Oz, so I borrowed a line from the main character, Dorothy. After announcing with much trepidation that I planned to move to Colorado to attend business college, I mimicked Dorothy's regret to her new friend, the scarecrow: "I think I'm going to miss you the most of all." Then I hugged him tightly and kissed him on the neck. It was the only time in my life that I have seen my father cry. Fighting back the tears, he managed to say that he was so angry with me he wanted to shake me, but he also loved me so much he just wanted to hold me forever and never let me go. I'm sure he wanted to hear, "There's no place like home. There's no place like home," but I couldn't say that. It crushed me to hurt him for he was as much an innocent pawn of my mother's religion as I.

In October of 1980, Lane's uncle volunteered to drive me to the Pittsburgh airport. Engaging my inherent common sense, I insisted Lane accompany us. On the way down we stopped at a gas station so Lane could use the restroom. I guess Lane's uncle felt I owed him something besides the $10 I supplied for gas. While Lane was gone, "Uncle Molester" tried to reach into the back seat several times and grab my breast. I fended him off, hitting his forearm repeatedly with my fist, sternly ordering him to stop. After a few unsuccessful attempts, he gave up. I still remember the sickening, smug look on that paunchy, dirty old man's face, and I empathized with how Lane must have felt to have his roaming hands violate the sanctity of her body. How pathetic and abominable that some older men must prey on young, vulnerable girls!

Despite the ongoing sexual abuse, Lane chose to trade in her self-esteem for a roof over her head. After I left Pennsylvania, she moved in with "Uncle Molester." How could she sell herself out to him? It was distressing to me that she didn't have the determination that I had to somehow seek out a better life. (Years later, I learned that she was still living with him, allowing herself to remain his dependent and victim.)

There is a saying I heard a long time ago that I've replayed in my mind for many years: *If you don't know what you want and where you are going, you will get next to nothing and end up nowhere.* I knew where I was going and what I wanted, glad to be leaving Pennsylvania behind in the gray clouds that day. It was my first airplane ride and although I was apprehensive, my spirits soared higher than that plane ever could!

Chapter 9: The Butterfly Takes Flight

You can't separate peace from freedom because no one can be at peace unless he has his freedom.

Malcolm X

It was late evening when my airplane landed in Colorado. As soon as I exited the plane, I was funneled through a very long, narrow corridor. In my mind the corridor symbolized my life—a long passage from which I had emerged, with a light shining brightly at the end. My aunt greeted me with a warm embrace. For the first time in ten years, I didn't feel alone.

Even though I was exhausted from the daylong commute, I was bursting with anticipation. In all my life, I've never known the wild abandonment I felt on that day, the sheer ecstasy.

In the night sky, the mountains cast a black silhouette on the horizon. All I could see were the streaks of headlights and streetlights en route to my cousin's house. I had heard my aunt describe for years how beautiful Colorado was. Daylight couldn't come fast enough. I was quite anxious to explore my new surroundings. But first I'd finally get to meet my cousin, Jenelle, and her husband, Ben. Although my aunt spoke of them often in her letters, these strangers were about to become my new family in Colorado.

Upon stepping into my cousin's contemporary, tri-level home, her two dogs, Pook and Dingbat, greeted me with sloppy licks along the tips of my fingers. Pook was a hyper West Highland White Terrier and Dingbat was a mellow, blissful black and white Lhasa apso with a significant under bite. As you might guess, Dingbat wasn't the brains in the family, but she was certainly adorable. (In later years, I would come to have dogs, Scruffy and Rags, that resembled them, and I'm sure my selection was no mere coincidence.)

Their house seemed so modern and polished compared to the farmhouse where I grew up. Older houses have dirty door handles and walls, scuffed baseboards and dirt that has been trapped for years in the windowsills. However, this house was different. It was *new*.

As I walked in, the formal living room appeared off to the right. Straight ahead, tucked around the corner, was the most compact kitchen I had ever seen. (Conversely, most farmhouses have gigantic kitchens to allow room for canning many acres of produce and vegetables.) The family room was situated down a few steps, to the left of the kitchen. I had never heard of a family room or a formal dining room before. Where I grew up, we had a living room with modest furniture and a simple kitchen with a table and chair ensemble located just a few feet from the sink and trash can. I thought, "Someday, I'll have a nice place like this!" (I never did buy into the Witnesses' philosophy that one must live in poverty, accepting the minimum in material possessions, in order to gain the Divine Being's favor.)

Jenelle, petite with cropped brunette hair, physically resembled my sister; however, she was more bubbly and energetic, like me. Ben towered over Jenelle and was dark, muscular and handsome. I noted that he looked a lot like the late actor, Christopher Reeves, and he shared with me that they had known each other in college.

After introductions were made, my aunt took me to my bedroom so I could unpack. Unlike my first apartment in Pennsylvania, I now had *a real bed* with soft, cotton sheets to sleep on and a fluffy pillow to cradle my head. Most importantly, for the first time in my entire life, I didn't have to share my bedroom with anyone else (except, occasionally, Pook and Dingbat). I drifted off in quiet slumber that night hugging my pillow with both a sense of excitement and mild trepidation.

My aunt and I decided to go sightseeing the next day. The beauty of the Rocky Mountains was everything she had described, and I was in awe of the open space in Colorado. In some places, you could see for fifty miles or more, a sharp contrast to the rolling hills of Pennsylvania where every hill blocked your view of the next. Colorado gave you a true sense of what it must have been like to live back in the 1800s, before today's large cities and suburban tract housing dotted the plains.

Colorado's brown terrain, dust and tumbleweeds gave the state its western flavor. In contrast, Pennsylvania's hillsides, a lush cucumber green, and fresh manure aromas wafting through the air, produced the state's farmland aura. Although Colorado was arid, I absolutely relished the low humidity and absence of pests. How nice it was to be able to walk outside without having swarms of bugs fly into my mouth and up my nose! As a young child, I remember all too well the locust plagues in the East that blanketed the roads with dead insects. (My most vivid bug memory is of my cousin Punchy dining on live locusts to freak me out.) Wasps, yellow jackets, and honeybees were everywhere in Pennsylvania. I could count on getting stung by a bee nearly every summer. But in twenty-three years, I've never been stung by a bee in Colorado.

All kinds of wildlife—elk, foxes, coyotes and rabbits—grazed in pastures right along the road. It was not uncommon to drive within ten feet of a herd of elk. For years my father had scoured the forests of Pennsylvania during hunting season trying to find game. It was a laborious task for him to even spot anything. When I saw how abundant wildlife was in Colorado, I thought of my father and how he would have found Colorado to be a hunter's paradise.

The most amazing thing to me was the sky. It was an unadulterated baby blue with absolutely no clouds in sight. In Pennsylvania, gray clouds usually blanketed much of the landscape, making even the sunniest summer day seem dingy and gloomy. If there was a heaven, it had to look like Colorado! Feeling the warmth of the sun shining on my face just intensified the optimism I held in my heart. It was what I needed to start a new chapter in my life.

While shopping with my aunt that day, I found a poster with the picture of a gray kitten on it that closely resembled my old cat, Mac. The fuzzy animal was lying in a small flowerpot, all four legs draped over the edges of the petite pot, as it dozed in blissful slumber. The caption underneath read, "When you are at peace with yourself, any place is home." When I saw that poster, I knew I had to buy it. I had been in Colorado less than twenty-four hours, but I had finally found peace...and home.

Later that day we visited a business college in Denver where I registered for the winter semester and applied for a student loan, which hurled me thousands of dollars into debt. My aunt agreed to purchase my books each semester as a separate loan. It was frightening to make such significant financial commitments, but I realized I needed to invest in my future.

The academic excellence that I strived for in high school paid huge dividends for me in college. I was skilled enough to test out of two entry-level classes (typing and English grammar), which permitted me to either indulge myself in two free hours during the day or take two electives instead. I chose to make the most of my education (and financial obligations) and take the two electives. (And, no, plumbing class was not on the list!)

That first week, my fear of using the public bus system came to fruition. After a particularly exhausting day at school, I boarded the public bus heading north instead of south. Forty-five minutes into the ride I arrived at the last remote stop. Of course, nothing looked familiar because I was at the wrong end of town! Darkness was falling and panic set in. I eventually managed to get on a bus going south, arriving home several hours late. Ever since, I've had a phobia about negotiating unfamiliar territory. I am by no means cured, even today. But it's a fear I am working hard to overcome.

Halfway through my last semester, I was offered a part-time job as a file clerk in downtown Denver. It would have been so easy for me to keep the door closed because the unknown was knocking on the other side. Negotiating a bus system in the suburbs (and getting lost!) was one thing, but finding my way around a busy metropolis seemed downright terrifying. Fortunately, I had the courage to face my fears. It was the same courage I found to feed my dogs in the dark and the same courage I mustered to take a stand against my mother and her religious cohorts.

My typical college day was grueling. After attending classes from 8:00 a.m. until 2:00 p.m., I'd take a bus downtown and work for an insurance company from 3:00 to 5:00 p.m. Once home, I had domestic chores plus between two and six hours of homework every night. To keep from getting behind, I started my assignments on the bus, barely lifting my head to take in the beautiful scenery. After transferring to yet another bus to get home, I would start dinner, throw in some laundry, clean up the house and wait for Jenelle and Ben to get home around 7 or 8. After dinner, I would finish any remaining homework and fall into bed around midnight, exhausted.

On weekends I babysat three young children (the oldest was seven) for a doctor and his wife. I usually worked between ten and twenty hours and could earn $20-$30. Bus fare was about $12 a week, which took a huge bite out of my earnings. After putting another $5 in Ben's truck for gas (he kindly allowed me to borrow it), I had enough money budgeted to buy a package of crackers each day for lunch and to purchase incidentals such as shampoo and tampons.

The next day I was up at 6 a.m. and at it all over again. Despite the overwhelming demands on my time, I loved every minute of my chaotic life and thrived on the adrenaline and excitement.

Amazingly enough, the bloody stumps at the tips of my fingers disappeared. My self-mutilation abruptly ended, even though I had been biting my nails to the quick for eight years. The stress I encountered in Colorado was not a negative stress. Rather, it was a satisfying, productive stress that left me feeling empowered and centered.

Ben was my mentor. He occasionally edited some of my homework and provided feedback. Since he was successful in corporate America, he was good at giving me pointers. His most noteworthy tip was, "Brenda, work on your grammar." Some days Jenelle actually made fun of me, and although she hurt my feelings, I realized I had a genuine problem. I had adopted what I affectionately call "Pennsylvania twang," and it took years for me to leave it completely behind. "Youns" was a favorite word, asking, "Do *youns* want to go to the store?" Or I would exclaim, "I told him I ain't got no patience for such thing!" Another was "Rid up the table." In some cases, I mispronounced words, "Can I *aaron* (iron) my blouse?" or "Let's *worsh* (wash) those clothes now." I must have sounded like a true hillbilly to them! I knew I had to become more articulate if I wanted to launch a successful business career in Colorado. (Little did I know that I'd eventually hone my skills enough to become a writer someday!)

I really admired Ben not only because he was a respected Rhodes scholar but also because he seemed to be accomplished in all aspects of his life. Ben was the consummate gentleman in every sense of the word and never said anything inappropriate to me. I envied my cousin and dreamt of someday finding such a wonderful husband. It was obvious to me that Ben was very devoted to Jenelle, and I had no intention of disrupting their bond. However, I must admit that I had absurd, unrealistic fantasies about Ben falling in love with me. I guess you could say I had a crush on him and did everything I could to curry his favor.

One scorching-hot day during the summer of 1981, Ben picked me up after babysitting and said he needed to make a quick trip to the store before we went home. A light bulb went on. A spontaneous, brilliant idea flashed through my brain. (Well, it *seemed* brilliant at the time.)

After he went into the store, I jumped out of the truck and dove into a nearby Baskin Robbins for two double-scooped, chocolate chip ice cream cones, one for him and one for me. I wanted to spend some of my babysitting money to show my appreciation for all he had done. As I sat in the truck anticipating his return, four minutes ticked by, then six, then eight, then ten. You get the picture. The ice cream began melting all over my clothes. I hadn't expected him to take so long! Not knowing what to do, I frantically started licking the sides of the cones in an attempt to contain the puddle that was rapidly developing in my lap. When the ice cream dribbled down the cone faster than my tongue could circle it, I began gobbling both ice cream cones down at once. At this point, I certainly didn't want him to catch me eating *two* ice cream cones. Heaven forbid that Ben view me as the fat pig

my brother had described! I had to get rid of the evidence—
pronto. The scene was beyond comical. By the time he came
out, I had devoured both cones. I tried my best to conceal the
stains on my clothes and the fact that I was feeling quite ill
(just imagine the brain freeze). I never told Ben about my
ordeal. The next time I felt especially generous, I just brought
home a pint instead (ice cream, not beer).

My first Christmas in Colorado was absolutely
spectacular. I'd waited ten years to celebrate a holiday with
family and whole-heartedly embraced the opportunity. Ben,
Jenelle and I drove to Colorado Springs and had a wonderful
dinner with my aunt and uncle. I felt like I had been reborn.

My aunt loved to cook and in addition to a fabulous
dinner she traditionally made a butter cream log cake for
dessert. The cake, laden with brown frosting and decorated to
look like a log with little meringue mushrooms on the sides,
reminded me of the innovative works of art I had concocted
for my father. As a teenager, I spent many hours in the
kitchen making one delicious dessert after another, often
decorating cakes with roses and beautiful borders. My father
had a special affinity for home-cooked food, and I loved to
surprise him with many delights to please his palate.

While Jenelle's home was indeed beautiful, my aunt's
home was absolutely exquisite. She lived in a custom-built,
two-story house on the side of a mountain in a very wealthy
neighborhood. The large entryway was paved with ceramic
tile. The living room showcased a huge, red brick fireplace
and mantel from which Christmas stockings hung. Her
kitchen alone was the size of my entire Pennsylvania
apartment. The dining room was the focal point,
showcasing how much my aunt loved to entertain. It had a
sliding glass door that led to a large redwood balcony,
overlooking downtown Colorado Springs, and a massive
crystal chandelier hanging over a beautifully carved cherry
wood dining table (which seated ten). During the holidays,

a freshly pressed tablecloth (uniquely embroidered for each occasion) adorned the table along with gold-plated utensils, festive china, and crystal water and wine glasses, perfectly arranged.

I spent many holidays in my aunt's home. With tears in her eyes, she'd put her arms around me and tell me she wanted me to feel like it was my home too. I loved her so much; she helped fill the void that had been left by my family. Yet, there was always something missing. I longed to have my mother, father, sister, nephews—and, yes, even my annoying brother—next to me on Christmas morning. Regardless, I stuffed those feelings inside and **hoped** that with each passing day it would get a little easier to accept the loss of my family. Unfortunately, it took years for me to realize that when you lose something precious to you, nothing can ever replace it. Even if you try to make substitution, the loss remains indefinitely. The sooner you can learn this lesson in life, the less suffering you will have. Denial imprisons. Acceptance, however, is liberating.

It was no accident that my aunt and I gravitated towards each other. Both of us had broken away from a poor country family to get an education. We both enjoyed baking and cooking. With red hair and fair skin (many people assumed I was her daughter), we even looked alike. And each of us had suffered a loss. I had lost my mother, and she a sister. Despite my aunt's efforts to have me stand on my own feet before leaving Pennsylvania, my parents blamed her nonetheless for my decision to leave and resented her for years.

The only gifts I remember getting that first Christmas were a diary and a set of blue-flowered plates, even though I received many more. Isn't it amazing that after being deprived of presents for so many years what mattered most to me was being with a family that loved me *unconditionally.* Nothing in this life rivals unconditional love and acceptance. Nothing.

All the while, both my father and mother pleaded with me to return home. I received dozens of letters from my mother, all filled with scripture, and although I repeatedly asked her to stop preaching to me, she wouldn't honor my wishes. Eventually, I resorted to returning her letters to her unopened. It pained me to have to be so harsh with her, but I didn't know what else to do. Asking her to respect my boundaries was like asking her to hold her breath indefinitely.

At this time in my life, I accepted that it wasn't really my mother who was reaching out to me—a mother who had nurtured me as a small child, who made sure I had my coat on when it was cold and that I was never hungry when I went to bed, a mother who kissed me repeatedly on the cheeks even though I pulled away with disgust and yelled "Eeewwwh!" This wasn't *my* mother. It was an icy apparatus built by Jehovah's Witnesses, driven to do its duty to try to recruit a "black sheep" back into the fold of the righteous. *This* alone was her mission. Once I recognized that an uncontrollable force was responsible for manipulating my mother—a force greater than our earthly bond—it was somewhat easier for me to accept our battered relationship and forgive her.

My dad, however, didn't fare so well. He remained a prisoner of denial for many years. When we spoke on the phone, all he could say was, "It's a shame you left, Brenda. You couldn't have been *that* unhappy." No matter what I said, he would not accept the truth. The guilt I felt for seeking to live my own life was a heavy burden I carried around for years.

There's no doubt that I was happier than I'd ever been, and I refused to allow anyone to squash that happiness. But I was so enmeshed in family battles, trying to hang onto who I needed to be and at the same time trying to change my family's mindset, that I didn't see that the train I was riding on was about to derail. In all my innocence and naiveté, I never imagined that by making one seemingly harmless choice, I would be switching tracks and sending my life into more chaos than I could ever imagine.

Chapter 10: Deaf, Dumb and Blind Dating

My grandmother's ninety. She's dating. He's about ninety-three. It's going great. They never argue. They can't hear each other.

Catherine Ladman

Less than five months after arriving in Colorado, I was introduced to a young man named Sean. This fateful encounter occurred as a result of a blind date set up by his mom. Sean had recently broken up with his girlfriend and was, understandably, depressed. His mom thought I was a "nice girl" who might be good for him. Anxious to go out on a second date, I apprehensively agreed.

A few nights later Sean telephoned me. Honestly, I wasn't at all impressed. Over the last year, I had become a progressively stronger, more confident woman and wanted to meet someone who was more like me. Sean didn't seem to have any direction in his life. Nevertheless, I rationalized, "What could it hurt?" and we agreed to meet.

A few days later this skinny young man with unruly, thin blonde hair, blue eyes, and a six-foot, two-inch frame knocked on my door. We struggled to make small talk for a few minutes. Then we decided to do what all first-time daters do when the conversation falters: go to a movie.

As I followed him out the door, I couldn't believe the wreck he called an automobile. His jeep, full of rust holes and sporting gray primer that covered the spotty canary paint job, looked like it came straight from the junkyard. The seats were ripped and the square hole in the floorboard perfectly framed the ground beneath my feet. I joked with him that the bottom was going to fall out as we were driving down the road, and we would find ourselves peddling the car with our feet like the Flintstones. It was filthy inside, cluttered with trash and scores of beer bottles. It took him several minutes to even clear the passenger seat of debris. I should have run for the mountains (because in Colorado, you have mountains, not hills), but decided to keep an open mind. After all, I had grown up with a mother who judged everyone. I certainly didn't want to become my mother!

We went to see *Xanadu*, a new release starring my favorite singer, Olivia Newton-John. The fact that we were going to see a show that I had been anticipating for weeks put me in a good mood.

After the movie, we went back to his place. All I can say is, "Holy cow!" I thought *I* had lived in poverty. His apartment was in deplorable condition. In addition to months of dust accumulation, there were piles of beer bottles and mounds of garbage overflowing from the trash can in his kitchen. However, the financial struggles I had endured in Pennsylvania helped me appreciate the fact that Sean was capable of living on his own. For a split second I rationalized away the scene, but then I noticed that Sean had a strange-looking glass object on his coffee table, one reeking with a nasty odor. Next to the glass bottle was what appeared to be dried-up parsley. When I asked him about the glass, he said it was a bong. I heard "bomb" and quietly wondered if he was involved in criminal activity. I hid my ignorance for a while until he later lit the "parsley" with a match. When I asked him what he was doing, he told me it was pot (marijuana). Illegal drugs? Was he kidding? I was mortified! Was it true that I had just been set up on a blind date with a drug user? By his mother nonetheless! What was she thinking? Surely she knew about her son's recreational habit. Did Jenelle and Ben know? What would my aunt think? And my highly sensitive mother would have a coronary if she found out! I had never seen pot before, so being exposed to it made me extremely uncomfortable. How dare Sean be so presumptuous and put me in such an awkward position on our first date! If I had had my own car, I would have left, but I was at Sean's mercy for transportation.

When he offered me a hit, I declined. All I could think was, "How can he smoke something that smells that foul?" I never considered for a moment that his lifestyle could foul up our lives. Like my mother who was approached by that Elder, I had no point of reference to know what type of person I was getting involved with. After all, I had only been on one date my whole life (Alex). However, because Sean seemed so kind, so sweet, I suppressed my feelings about the drugs and agreed to go out with him again. (This is why the chapter is titled, "Deaf, Dumb *and* Blind Dating.") I must admit that despite the initial shock, I was also strangely curious, proving that opposites do attract.

When my mother learned that I was dating Sean, she reminded me that dating outside The Truth is wrong. I knew that if she had issues with me dating a nonbeliever, then confiding in her that I was dating a druggie on top of it was probably completely out of the question. So with a mix of embarrassment topped off with a dash of fear, I said nothing about his lifestyle. It was my first moment as an enabler. In hindsight, perhaps that was part of the allure of dating Sean. Since my mother would never approve of *any* man I ever dated, it didn't matter what type of man Sean was. She didn't care whether I dated the pope or an ax murderer. It was all the same to her.

Despite my usual propensity for exercising common sense, I ignored all the warning signs because I knew Sean came from a good, respectable family. His mother was a schoolteacher and his father a lawyer, after all. My naiveté fooled me into believing that he was simply an undeveloped pupa with real potential. It was a big lesson to learn that you should never date or marry anyone for his or her alleged potential. Once again, I was about to learn how dangerous assumptions are and how easily one person could change my world forever.

Chapter 11: Taking an Honorable Stand

In August of 1981, my Colorado family attended my highly anticipated college graduation ceremony. Afterwards, one of the teachers stood up and announced that she had an Outstanding Student Award for someone with a flawless attendance and 4.0 average. When she called out my name, I was speechless. I knew I had done really well in school, but I had no idea I was the top student out of several hundred! Everyone patted me on the back as I sat there dumbfounded, immobilized in shock. My aunt nudged me to stand up, and I stumbled forward. Tears of pride steamed down my cheeks as I made my way up to the front of the room to accept the award. No one but me really knew the mountains I had figuratively—as well as literally—scaled to be given this fantastic recognition:

- Taking a difficult stand against the Jehovah's Witnesses and my mother
- Eating French fries for weeks to survive in a world outside my Jehovah's Witness cocoon
- Braving my first plane flight across the country with nothing but **hopes** and **dreams** in my pockets
- Moving in with complete strangers
- Maintaining several part-time jobs while attending college
- Traversing an unfamiliar city using a foreign bus system

And now I was graduating as top student in the secretarial field. What an incredible honor! Recognition or no recognition, one thing was certain. I had acquired the technical skills to ensure that I'd no longer have to flip burgers for a living or eat other people's garbage.

My mother may not have supported my move towards independence. However, I knew my father, a blue-collar worker, would have appreciated the merit of what I had accomplished, had he been able to witness my life as it unfolded that year. I had **hopes** that someday my dad would be proud to say that his little girl was the only one in our family to graduate from college.

**1981–Proudly displaying my certificate of
completion and award following my graduation
from business college.**

My struggles to rectify poverty through education
intensified the disrespect I felt towards my brother. When I
was nine years old, my brother was taking classes in college
but abandoned them when Mother coerced the family into
joining the Jehovah's Witnesses. Why would he turn his back
on such a valuable opportunity? The reason is simple:
Witnesses believe that higher education is ultimately a waste
of time. Instead, followers are encouraged to spend as much
of their free time in the door-to-door service as they possibly
can. They eagerly await the "New Order"—Armageddon—
which they anticipate any day now. (They've anticipated it

"any day now" for over a century!) Since Jehovah will be providing for all necessities of life in this New Order, who needs to know anything about computers, space travel or running a corporation?

While I concede that choosing to forego an education and enrich his life *is* my brother's choice—not a wise choice, in my opinion, but his choice nonetheless—it is more than this that fuels my less-than-forgiving attitude. What really provokes me is that my brother is malingering to provide the basics of food, clothing and shelter for his family. On the other hand, he is incredibly zealous in performing the ministry. He will devote countless hours trying to save us heathens, but he can't even save himself. Today, he lives in poverty with his wife in an old mobile home somewhere in rural Tennessee. My dad, who has worked incredibly hard performing manual labor all of his life, has become his financial wishing well. All my brother has to say is, "I wish I had some money to pay for..." and my father obliges. Instead of finding gainful employment, my brother has prostituted himself for the Jehovah's Witnesses. He can't see that, in selling himself to gain some advantage in the New Order, he has sacrificed the rudiments of *this* life.

Nearly every family in America has someone like my brother. There is always someone unwilling to give back to the world what they take from it. Likewise, nearly every family in America has someone like my father—someone who fosters dependency in another. At the time, however, I thought *I* was above all that. I couldn't understand how my father, a man with such strong work ethics, could allow his son to become a parasite. In time I learned that as I was calling the kettle black, I was actually boiling tea using the same recipe as my father. Once again, history was about to repeat itself, and I'd come to understand how someone could be compelled to financially support and, at the same time, cripple another's independence. (Be careful whom you judge, for you may, unknowingly, be gazing at yourself, indeed your very future, in the mirror.)

As soon as I graduated, I accepted a full-time junior secretarial position with Ben's company. It was the financial security I needed. Six months later, I was promoted, my company's first employee to learn word-processing software. While all the other administrative staff declined to tackle the unknown, this redhead actually rallied for the challenge. (I must admit, I was terrified.)

Soon thereafter, I answered an ad for a roommate and rented a duplex with another girl in one of the worst parts of Denver. In my naiveté, I didn't comprehend how dangerous this area was. While walking home from the bus stop one evening, several guys followed me from their pickup truck, making catcalls and taunting me. Each night I scurried home like a mouse evading its predator, **hoping** I'd survive long enough to find a safer place to live. I called this duplex home for a few months and, like so many other difficulties in my life, I somehow survived it.

Eventually I saved enough money to get my first car—a beautiful gray, sporty Capri. Its burgundy interior reminded me of those raspberries I had smashed in milk as a child. I felt fabulously chic sitting behind the leather-bound steering wheel. And like those raspberries, my first set of wheels gave me a sense of enjoyment and security not provided by the public bus system. Now I was truly liberated!

On this highway called life, where were my choices going to steer me? Although the world was still my oyster (and I had found a few pearls along the way), I **hoped** for even more. Like so many young adults who strike out on their own for the first time, I had big expectations but little experience to help guide me.

Chapter 12: Searching for Unconditional Love and Acceptance

Love can sometimes be magic. But magic can sometimes...just be an illusion.

Javan

My parents naturally thought I'd return to Pennsylvania once I finished college. When I received one hundred dollars in the mail (the first money I'd seen from them in over eighteen months), I knew they were trying to solidify their assumptions. Then came the offer I *could* resist. If I moved back to Pennsylvania and agreed to live with them, they'd help me find a job. So far, so good, right? Not so fast. I clearly saw their offer as bait set to entrap me. The tightly wound, nearly invisible string attached to their offer began to fray when my mother announced, "And you must start attending meetings at the Kingdom Hall again!" I declined without a second of hesitation. Nevertheless, I longed to pay a visit and show them the new me.

Now, if you've ever worked for an extended period of time without taking a single day of vacation or braved a blizzard for hours while waiting for a bus, you can appreciate it when I say that I really needed a break after graduation. Unfortunately, I knew I would have to continue to work nonstop for at least another twelve months in order to accrue a week's worth of vacation and save enough money for plane fare. But it was a sacrifice I was willing to make. For more than a respite for myself, I longed to hold my nephews in my arms again and plant kisses on their chubby cheeks.

When I finally arrived at the Pittsburgh airport a year later, my father met me with tears in his eyes and an obvious hesitancy. It had been almost two years since we'd seen each other. We walked to the parking lot and climbed into his truck. Before turning the ignition key, he paused and gazed at me. I could tell he was struggling to say something important and that his tears weren't just happiness to see me, but also sorrow.

"I didn't want to tell you this before, because I figured you wouldn't fly back here to see us. But your sister won't let you see her kids because she thinks you will influence them in some way. She won't see you either." I stared into his hazel eyes with morbid disbelief. Anger pulsated throughout my body. After I stopped reeling from the shock, I spouted, "Dad, how can *I* possibly influence my sister's young children to turn against her?" He shook his head and shrugged his shoulders. Once again, the logic of the Jehovah's Witnesses was at work in its own twisted fashion. My sister's ostracism of me seemed like retaliation. She was branding me as a vile, infectious virus when she knew nothing about me. At that moment, I realized I'd never see my sister or her children again. Not that year, not next year.

Never.

My nephews would be isolated from their aunt (just as I'd been forbidden to correspond with mine) because of my sister's ridiculous fears and need to control them. History was repeating itself.

After the nearly two-hour drive into the country, we finally approached the old farmhouse. I saw my best friend's car parked roadside. Cindy had been driving back and forth, anxiously awaiting my arrival. We ran to each other, embracing and shrieking with delight, much like we had in our previous encounters with Alex. We chatted briefly then made plans to get together the next day. A few yards away I could see my mother's smile waning. She appeared uncomfortable. I was, after all, speaking to a "nonbeliever." As Mother and I began walking towards the house, she commented about my bad associations. I matter-of-factly informed her that I would be spending some of my visit with old school friends. A pained, constipated look came over her face. At that moment, the truth about our relationship was forced upon her. She could no longer suffocate me nor grab onto that symbolical umbilical cord and yank me back, as she was once accustomed to doing. Although I had accomplished so much since leaving my Pennsylvania home two years earlier, *this* conversation was the defining moment in my life when I realized that I, Brenda, had arrived. The little farm girl had become an adult.

Once inside, my mother called my brother and his wife on the telephone. I found it interesting to note that unlike Cindy my brother was not anxiously awaiting my arrival and had to actually be summoned. About fifteen minutes later, he meandered from my coveted spot with his wife in tow. Everyone's demeanor was very tentative; we all could have suffocated from the high concentration of angst in the air, even with a steady flow of oxygen. Nevertheless, I made a whole-hearted attempt to be upbeat, loving and humorous. After all, laughter is the best way to harvest oxygen.

The next day I rejoiced at meeting several of my old girlfriends. The greatest compliment I could have received was when one of them noted, "Geez, Brenda. You don't sound like us no more." I just smiled. The Pennsylvania twang was gone! "Geez. Thanks, youns," was all I could say.

On the way back to the airport, my father kept badgering me: "It wasn't that bad, was it, Brenda?" (He was referring to my years living as a Witness.) Even though I had tried countless times to explain how unhappy I was, my dad still lived in a state of denial. He longed to see me shred the plane ticket in my hand and hear me say that I'd forsake Colorado. But I couldn't. I wouldn't. Dorothy's line in "The Wizard of Oz"—"There's no place like home"—meant Colorado to me, not Pennsylvania.

I didn't want to hurt my father, but I wanted to impress upon him just how fanatical Mother had become. I wanted him to find some peace with the alternate path I had chosen. I wanted him to learn, as I had, that acceptance is liberating. I looked him squarely in the eyes and with steadfast conviction declared, "Dad, if the Jehovah's Witnesses told Mother to **murder** her entire family, like the Jim Jones' cult did, and twisted some scripture to justify that it was the right thing to do, you know she would have killed us all in an instant." My father bowed his head and tears welled up in his eyes. While he couldn't bring himself to verbally acknowledge I was right, he knew I was. With raw passion he hugged his little girl and offered that he'd literally give his right arm to make us a family again. If only he could do something. *Anything*. Dear daddy. Poor, dear daddy...

We sat quietly in his truck for a few moments, absorbing the deafening silence that permeated the space between us. Before I left, I had one burning question to ask. You see, Jehovah's Witnesses don't believe in blood transfusions and many have let family members die as a result of that belief. (They once also felt the same way about vaccinations but then quietly changed their policy.) I wanted to know what he would have done had I ever needed a blood transfusion during my childhood. All along, my dad yielded to Mother's religious beliefs. Would he have saved my life if push came to shove? Would he have gone to bat for me when confronted by the Elders? Would he have faced the consequences from the rest of our family in order to save his daughter? I desperately needed to hear that someone in my family valued *me* more than that man-made religion. With sorrow in his eyes, he assured me that he would have stood his ground, but his hesitancy to respond gave me nauseating pause. Sadly, I wasn't convinced.

We kissed good-bye and I boarded the plane, choking back the tears. It was far more agonizing to leave him behind this time. I desperately wanted to smuggle him into my suitcase and take him back to Colorado with me so he could experience my happiness for himself. I wept for over an hour as I made my way home, never anticipating that, time and again, my own happiness would soon come under attack, forcing me to ask myself where happiness really comes from.

Once I was back in Colorado, I foolishly dabbled in disaster. My dates with Sean always wound up the same way, with him getting wasted from chugging beer and smoking pot. Because all of his friends did the same thing, I thought that maybe *I* was the peculiar one. I reasoned that if I could free myself from the emotional prison my parents had erected, surely I could save him, too. Besides, wouldn't he just grow out of it and mature at some point? Didn't his mother suggest that I would be good for him?

You know the cliché: "The love of a good woman can change a man." What a bunch of malarkey! It should read: "The love of a good woman can change a man...into a fetus." After all, aren't we just promoting dependence when we "take care of our man?" It's tough enough struggling every day to hang onto our own sanity. Must we become muddled in *their* every emotional crisis as well? If they aren't fully developed yet (i.e., if they're in the fetal stage), don't we automatically wind up doing everything for them? Don't we get angry for them, love for them, be responsible for them, get jobs for them, cry for them, plan their vacations, set up their schedules and promote their happiness (although fleeting)? I'm sure anyone who has lived with an addict knows exactly what I'm talking about.

Along with Sean's substance abuse came financial irresponsibility. Rarely did he have the money to buy inexpensive birth control, yet he could routinely drop a hundred dollars on marijuana like it was pocket change. If we wanted to go anywhere or do anything, I had to plan for it. I had to pay for it. I became the giver, he the taker.

Eventually I broke up with Sean when I realized that I wanted more from a relationship than he could ever offer. I knew in my heart that I deserved a knight in shining armor, not a stoned, incoherent peasant, but with my novice dating and social skills, I wasn't sure how to find one.

After the breakup, I feared dating. Given how easily and quickly Sean captivated my heart and drew me into his world, I didn't have much confidence that I would be able to avoid a relationship with anyone who was bad for me. Unfortunately, men like Sean seemed to abound everywhere. I found myself in the same situation as my mother when those "nice" Jehovah's Witnesses knocked on her door—needy and confused. My emotional bank account was empty, and I desperately needed someone to make a deposit. I wanted a man, a good man, to love me.

A coworker of mine, Norma, suggested we room together. With a steady, full-time job under my wing, I was able to improve my financial situation and escape my unsafe, dreadful neighborhood. Our new pad was located in the western suburbs of Denver in a new, peaceful neighborhood. We lived on the second floor and had a beautiful view of the foothills, which were covered with coniferous vegetation and red, jagged boulders. Norma and I became the best of friends.

Soon I was able to save enough money to purchase a new king-size waterbed and nightstand and six-piece living room ensemble. In less than two years on my own, I was completely self-sufficient, a far cry from my early days in Pennsylvania when I had only one lamp and one beanbag chair to my name.

Every Saturday night like clockwork, Norma and I hit the Denver dance clubs, always searching for Mr. Right, but usually going home early in the morning disappointed. Despite my dating phobia, I met and courted two men. The first was an Italian stud who did not hesitate to "bum" money from me every chance he got (déjà vu, Sean). He habitually picked me up with his new Camaro running on empty, then asked me to pay not just for dinner but for gas so he could get home. I must have had a sign plastered on my forehead that said, "Take advantage of this gullible country bumpkin." I wised up after I learned that he snorted his paycheck up his nose (cocaine). I must say I was very pleased with myself when I found the courage to break up with him after only a few dates.

The second man I dated, Jim, reminded me of Ben. Jim was one year younger than me, handsome, accomplished in his career and drug-free. He was very generous, frequently buying dresses or teddy bears to surprise me. Jim was an incredible, passionate lover. Some weekends we immersed ourselves in each other, spending the entire day in bed, caressing and loving. He taught me a lot about sex, and I fell head over heels in love with him. Unfortunately, our three-month relationship ended prematurely because we were both just too emotionally immature to deal with conflict. Devastated, I beached myself like a whale for months afterwards and decided to forego dating for a long, long time. Fate, however, had other plans. High tide was about to intervene and sweep this beached whale right back out to sea.

The year was now 1982. My cousin and Sean's mother threw a birthday party for themselves at the horse stables where they worked. I was looking forward to the party, as Dan Fogelberg, the famous folk singer from Colorado, planned to attend. Dan knew my cousin through their mutual love of horses. Starstruck, I asked him the stupidest question once his song started playing: "Do you ever get sick of hearing yourself sing?" What can I say; I was only twenty and it showed.

Dan wasn't the only guest at the party that short-circuited my brain. When I saw Sean walk through the door, I felt like I had entered the *Twilight Zone*. Part of me still loved him, but common sense told me that talking to him would be like stirring up a red anthill. My aunt—a very assertive woman who wanted to be politically correct with this family—nudged me his direction. She insisted I at least acknowledge him. I scoffed and resisted as long as I could but eventually caved. Unfortunately, neither one of us foresaw how that single action would alter the course of my life. Sean and I talked and as we did, I found myself magnetically drawn to him. Jim's departure had left me quite vulnerable.

The next day I found a single rose and book entitled, "Happiness is Being With You" attached to my apartment door. Sean was a long shot from being husband material, but he did make me feel very special and loved. At that point in my life, it was exactly what I craved.

Over the next year, Sean and I dated exclusively. Despite his questionable lifestyle, I eventually suggested we live together. While our relationship certainly wasn't perfect, cohabitation just made financial sense. We both needed roommates. (Norma, who unexpectedly found herself pregnant, moved back in with her family.) My aunt wasn't so supportive. This was the beginning of the end to our relationship.

My life with Sean grew into co-dependency because it was the two of us against the world (or so it seemed). Sean battled his addictions and I battled my parents. It was our bond. And our demons always seemed to be lurking right around the corner wearing polyester suits.

One lazy Saturday morning in particular comes to mind. It was December 1982. Sean and I had just made love and were lying in bed when we heard a knock at the door. Assuming it was the landlord, I jumped up, loosely threw on a robe, and flung open the front door. There stood two Jehovah's Witnesses with briefcases in hand and tentative smiles on their faces. "Brenda?" they asked. "Yes," I replied apprehensively. "We are here to provide loving assistance," the eldest one flatly announced, just like a recording. How horrifying! When I heard those words, I realized my mother had, from a thousand miles away, invaded my apartment complex by sending Elders to lecture me. My horror quickly turned to anger, and I foolishly tried to argue with them about the validity of their beliefs. (Never argue with a Jehovah's Witness. You would fare better to extract your own tooth while attempting to maintain your balance on a unicycle... blindfolded...perched on a tightrope.) As I stood there at the door, I could feel sweat pouring from my brow after our rather frisky round of hot, passionate lovemaking. Their timing was impeccable. Years later, Sean and I still snickered about that incident.

True to form, the Elders visit *again* forever changed my life. A few weeks later, I received a letter in the mail:

January 4, 1983

Dear Brenda,

In our files we have your card as being one of the baptized members of Jehovah's Witnesses. In order to keep the files up to date, we would like to make the following inquiry.

Do you still want to be known as one of Jehovah's Witnesses? If so, we would like to make arrangements to have the local congregation give you loving assistance. Please inform us of your answer. You may use the self-addressed stamped envelope enclosed for your reply.

Your servants for Jehovah,

NF
BA
JB

At this point in my life, I was still an emotional time bomb ready to explode, sick and tired of their "loving assistance" and self-righteousness. I abruptly shot back:

Why would I "<u>still</u>" want to be known as one of Jehovah's Witnesses if I never considered myself to be one in the first place?

As a 10-year old <u>child</u>, my baptism meant nothing more to me than something Mother wanted me to do. Therefore, in essence, I was never baptized and am not a "baptized Jehovah's Witness." To sum it all up—NO!

Brenda

I wasn't sure, but I suspected that their letter was a ploy to determine if I should be excommunicated. With my somewhat ambiguous reply, I was actually hoping that it would be difficult for them to expel me. After all, how do you take something away from someone, such as a membership, if they never had it to begin with? It's not that I wanted to be linked with them. I was simply trying to prevent permanent severance from my family by throwing a little confusion into the letter. It didn't work.

Less than two months later, precisely on my twenty-first birthday, my mother telephoned to deliver the devastating news. Without a hint of emotion, she announced that she, my sister and my brother would *never* speak to me again. Although I'd expected the shunning for some time, it still felt like a battering ram had just pummeled me square in the abdomen. With dignity and grace I simply replied, "Well, OK, then. Have a good life." And with that, my mother, brother and sister walked out of my life forever. [6]

Sean had supported me emotionally through all the conflict I had had with my mother during the previous two years. He provided a shoulder for me to cry on when I needed it. With my mother out of the picture I thought my anxiety would subside, but our feuding had taken such a toll on me that I continued to have nightmares. I often woke up sobbing, my clothing drenched in sweat.

In an attempt to cope with the emotional mayhem swirling through my brain, I sought out an employee assistance counselor. I needed to come to grip with the fact that most of my family would never again be a part of my life. Somehow I had the insight to choose a healthy outlet instead of a destructive one. (It would have been so easy to sling back the booze and numb the pain as Sean frequently did.) I attended several sessions with a therapist over many months, seeking to gain some insight into my

---

[6] To this day, I have trouble understanding how Jehovah's Witnesses can lovingly call each other, even strangers, "brother" and "sister," yet turn their backs on their own family members. There is some peculiar, warped contradiction in that.

emotions. Through it all, I learned a new word: dysfunctional. My family and Sean were not healthy—and neither was *I*. I had become an enabler, someone who excused and tolerated—even promoted—unhealthy behavior. Like my father, I had fostered dependency in another.

My relationship with my aunt continued to deteriorate. Her intervention to help me create a new life for myself in Colorado created a debt I felt I could never repay. When she proudly introduced me to her friends, she frequently explained, "This is my niece from Pennsylvania. We educated her." Although I greatly appreciated what she had done for me, her comment felt condescending and seemed to be self-serving. It didn't seem she was giving *me* the credit for all of my hard-earned accomplishments.

When I first moved to Colorado, I was in awe of everything my aunt said and did. I adored her and she knew it. As I began to mature, however, I began to see her as a fallible human being and sometimes questioned how she was treating me. I sensed she didn't want to lose my adoration, but it was an inevitable part of my growth process. In some ways, I think she was envious of the place in my heart that Sean occupied and frustrated at her inability to continue to influence my life. Perhaps she could see the destructive path I was walking with Sean. After all, she too had been married to an alcoholic. Over time I came to understand that it was probably her own insecurities she was fighting. I believe that as my own confidence and sense of identity continued to blossom, she became less and less secure about her role in our relationship and the crevasse between us widened. To be honest, I wasn't the best company either during that tumultuous time in my life, and she probably found it easier to distance herself from me.

Whatever the reason for our alienation, the trips to see my aunt became a one-way street that became more and more bumpy. Holidays soon had the festivity sucked right out of them. The joy I had known when I first moved to Colorado—being able to experience holiday celebrations with loving family—turned into a malicious tug-of-war. On Thanksgiving and Christmas we tried to compromise by spending a few hours with Sean's parents at their house, then driving a hundred miles to Colorado Springs to spend some time with my aunt and uncle. Despite the juggling act, I felt like we could not adequately please any of them. "Do you have to go *already*? Can't you spend more time with *us*?" were the standard questions of the day.

On more than one occasion, my aunt gave her daughters holiday leftovers but completely overlooked me. This took me back to the days when my mother bragged about how she had taken stew or pies to my sister, never offering any to me. Like Santa's proverbial lump of coal, the weight of her actions and words became more difficult for me to bear.

During her trips to Denver to visit Jenelle, my aunt seemed to always have an excuse for why she couldn't make it to *our* home to visit with us. Once again, I felt like I was getting conditional love from a family member. There were many such incidents, none of which I will go into because I don't want to dishonor my aunt. I really do love her. She played a tremendous role in bringing my future into focus and, for that, I will be eternally grateful. However, at the time I didn't realize how many emotionally unhealthy people surrounded me, influencing my life.

With all the mundane choices we make each and every day, it's amazing how just one choice, one circumstance, can alter a person's life forever. I often wonder how different my life might have been had my aunt allowed me to live with *her* in Colorado Springs while I attended college. Sean and I may have never met and the pool of single men from my aunt's circle of friends might have offered me a better opportunity for a healthy relationship with a man. Or perhaps constant exposure to my aunt's negativity and callous behavior may have sent me into a deeper abyss. "What if's" aside, I had to play with the cards I had been dealt.

My life was about to turn into a royal flush, and I'm not referring to the best hand in poker. Think back to my days as a "plumberette," and you'll appreciate the analogy.

Chapter 13: Come to Jesus Meeting

We cannot change anything until we accept it. Condemnation does not liberate, it oppresses.

C. G. Jung

The years that followed were bittersweet. While the frustration of dealing with my mother was pretty much history, dealing with my father's emotions became yet another battle I had to charge through. Although he still talked to me, I dreaded our conversations and cringed when the phone rang.[7]

My departure from our dysfunctional family had left my father in a state of turmoil, which became quite apparent in the guilt trips he pawned off. He'd ask, "Would it hurt you to go to a few meetings again and bring some peace to our

---

[7] My father could speak to me because he had never received baptism eleven years earlier when the rest of the family took that plunge. He retained his right to be a part of my life. I could empathize with how difficult it was for my father to be a fence sitter. While he maintained ties with me, he was very torn. He also felt loyal to my sister, brother, mother and their religion. He thought it was his duty to unite our family. It was a precarious ball that no parent should ever have to juggle.

family?" (as though I alone was somehow responsible for our family's perverted dynamics). The mere thought of stepping foot into a Kingdom Hall, however, sent waves of post-traumatic anxiety throughout my body. To me, my father's comment was like telling a woman who has been beaten, "Go back to your abusive husband. It wasn't that bad, was it? Sure, he broke a few bones, but for goodness sakes, you're still alive, aren't you?"

For the first time in our lives, my father and I argued. He became the communication vessel for my mother so she could cleverly continue her preaching. Once, as father started quoting scriptures to me (something he'd never done before), I suggested to him that he was simply parroting Mother. My bulls eye remark was not well received. He fired back a heated letter to me, stating that he had a mind of his own. I guess the truth sometimes hurts for if it hadn't been true, he wouldn't have become so defensive. After that confrontation, he no longer allowed my mother to pull his puppet strings.

For a relatively healthy young man (mid-50s), he obsessed about dying. Nearly every conversation was riddled with, "Someday soon I'll be gone; I don't have many years left." This was difficult for me to hear. Was he willing himself to die, was he trying to impose remorse upon me for my actions, or was he simply trying to prepare me for the inevitable someday? His choice to wallow in depression and play the victim broke my heart.

While I loved my father immensely, his lack of empathy and constant whining about my "sinful" lifestyle started to get on my nerves. After several years of listening to my father's misguided opinion—that I had no valid reason to leave the Witnesses—I decided to confront him directly, once and for all. I call it my "Come to Jesus Meeting." I knew I'd risk losing him along with the rest of my family. He was, after all, the only link in our family chain that allowed me to know whether my mother and siblings were dead or alive. But confrontation was necessary. Otherwise, I knew we'd drift apart and never find each other again. The letter I crafted to Dad stated, in part:

> I've sent you some of the poems I've written through the years. As a parent, I'm sure it's hard to believe or accept that your child was so unhappy in his/her teens that suicide was seriously considered. That's why, on the phone and many times before, you say I was "imagining" things or "it wasn't that bad." I'm sending these poems so you'll see just how bad it was...

> I've been told by many people that if they had gone through what I did, they would have either had a nervous breakdown or hated their parents and never have spoken to them again. I almost wish I could be that way—to hate you both—because it would make things much easier to accept. But I can't do that. I'll always love you both and hope someday that Mother comes to realize what a very special, loving daughter she just tossed aside.

I realized it would take more than a letter to help my dad accept the choices I'd made. Although we don't physically resemble each other, we are very much alike in the way we think, so I knew he'd hold out some hope that I might eventually return. To counter any false hopes, I assured him that I'd never be a Jehovah's Witness again. I appealed to the intellectual dad I knew and loved: "Why would I want to be part of any so-called loving religion that forces a mother to make a choice between her own life (eternal life) and the life of her child (i.e., being a part of that child's life now)? I'd never choose my life over my child's life! Yet, that is precisely what I'd be expected to do if I stayed in the Jehovah's Witnesses' faith for the sake of my family and *my* child decided to leave the religion someday. It's inconceivable!"

I informed my dad that he should read my poetry and short story, *All Alone in the World*, and then decide whether or not Mother should even know it exists. I knew my words wouldn't change her convictions, and I saw no point in rubbing salt into her wounds, as she had so callously done to me.

For the first time in many years, my sister broke her silence and sent me a letter of reprimand. Obviously, she and Mother gobbled up everything I had written. She felt my "Come to Jesus Meeting" was insensitive and disrespectful. Maybe it was, but after years of being bombarded with abuse, shunning, and guilt, I was at a junction in my life. I had to decide whether to try to make peace with the one remaining family member I had as he symbolically tore into my fragile wings or simply fly away forever. My sister always had my family's support, love and respect. She never longed for acceptance or freedom. She had absolutely no right to judge me.

My strategy worked. I sensed an immediate change in my father. He came to grips with the fact that I could never live again as a Witness. Even he couldn't argue that when a child fantasizes about killing her parents (or herself), she is *not* a happy camper.

Although my relationship with my father mended as a result of that confrontation, the relationship I fostered with Sean was about to further hamper my flight. This time, however, something would be different. My wings wouldn't simply become torn, they'd become nearly detached.

Chapter 14: "Happily Ever After"

My relationship with Sean can be likened to a pea-sized snowball rolling downhill, collecting not only snow but also undesirable debris—sticks, leaves and perhaps a little doggie doo-doo as well. After three years of living together, I was too enmeshed in the life I had built with Sean to end it. I knew I'd never be able to roll Sean into a happy, wholesome, pearly white snowman. Yet I hated the idea of starting over with someone else. My earlier concern—would I have the strength to end a relationship with someone who was bad for me—materialized with Sean.

Sean would have been happy living together forever, but after four years I wanted a permanent relationship in my life. With my mother and siblings gone, I hungered for a family. I basically gave Sean an ultimatum: "Marry me or hit the road, Jack!" This wasn't how I had envisioned a proposal. As a little girl you read about the princess being swept up by her lover and carried to a castle in the clouds. At a minimum you **hope** the man you love will get down on bended knee and lovingly propose with a ring in hand. You never imagine that you will someday have to rope your man like a steer and drag him to the ground. Knowing I coerced Sean into marriage made the whole arrangement bittersweet.

Sean's investment in our future was nil. Like a good little enabler, I played the role of the financially responsible one. On the other hand, Sean spent hundreds of dollars every month on his mechanic's tools—as well as on foreign substances that polluted his body and mind (cigarettes, alcohol and drugs). I wasn't happy with this arrangement, and we had many heated discussions about it, but I **hoped** this would change after we married. I even paid for my own engagement ring. Talk about dimwitted! If the man I loved wouldn't scrape together a few dollars to prevent an unplanned pregnancy, how in the world would he ever reimburse me for a $900 engagement ring? Who was this woman making such assumptions? My common sense must have taken a vacation.

We married in June of 1985. Like most weddings, it had its ups and downs, both in the planning stage and in the culmination. The biggest disappointment came when Jenelle chose to forego one of the most important days in my life so she could participate in a horse show instead. I was absolutely crushed. Her decision revealed how little our relationship meant to her, even though I had embraced her like a sister (at this point my biological sister was no longer speaking to me).

As I scanned the audience of one hundred guests, I could easily locate my aunt and uncle and *three* friends. The remaining ninety-five guests were there for Sean. As expected, none of my Pennsylvania family was there.[8] This cold reality cast a dark shadow over my big day. I recalled my father's advice when he cautioned years earlier, "Don't depend on friends, Brenda. Friends come and go, but your family will always be there for you. Blood is thicker than water." He just failed to mention, sadly, that he wasn't talking about *our* family!

The next few years were tough, but as long as I buried my head in the sand like the proverbial ostrich and refused to acknowledge that my husband was an alcoholic and drug addict, we were fine. I had survived childhood by living a lie. Mother and the Witnesses trained me well to live with dysfunction and suppress my feelings. As a result, many years of my life eroded away while I foolishly rode in a car with a drunken driver—a man who couldn't comprehend that he was endangering my life as well as his own. Frequent episodes of ritualistic self-abuse unfolded before my eyes as I witnessed Sean's descent into deeper patterns of self-loathing and depression. Years crept by while I held Sean's hand throughout the night, begging him to not slit his wrists as I frantically tried to help him find a reason to live.

When I realized Sean wasn't changing as I had **hoped**, I sought out a marriage counselor. After several sessions, the counselor made a startling prediction: "You'll divorce this man someday." I impetuously cast her crystal ball aside. Me—divorce Sean someday? We had married until "death do us part." Wasn't it the counselor's job to fix Sean? Surely she could see I had done my part by getting him to her office in the first place. How dare she assume she couldn't help us!

---

[8] Remarkably, although mother wouldn't talk to Sean while we were engaged and refused to attend our wedding, she still assumed that she had somehow earned the right to bombard Sean with literature and preach to him. When we returned from our honeymoon, we found her religious magazines in our mailbox, addressed to Sean.

The counselor was clearly frustrated with Sean. He lacked motivation to make any changes in his life—showing up inebriated for the sessions and refusing to do any of the assignments—but she obviously didn't love him like I did, nor did she have the patience I had (and so the enabler in me reasoned). In hindsight I see that the counselor saw the writing on the wall, the something in Sean, the something in me that I could not. I still had so much to learn. Many years of lies and dysfunction held me in this psychological prison before I finally woke up and smelled the very black coffee.

As a young adult, I learned a valuable lesson: No matter what methods I utilized, no matter how many tears I shed, no matter how much I loved, hated, yelled, reasoned or pleaded, I couldn't change the man I loved any more than I could change my mother. The reality is, you can't change anyone but yourself.

For a fleeting moment in time, I held fast to the illusion that all my pleadings had finally paid off. My murky mirage produced a man who had taken his life back. Oh, how I longed for it to be true for I loved Sean dearly! Sean stopped using drugs and alcohol and landed a better job. For the first time in our lives our salaries were comparable, and I had **hopes** Sean would contribute more to our relationship. I naively assumed our struggles were over.

By September 1987 I saved $5,000 for a down payment on a new home. The three-bedroom, two-bathroom tri-level with all new appliances, vaulted ceilings, wood stair railings, two-car garage and large backyard became our pride and joy. The new house smell, which I've since determined is really just glue, paint fumes, and other potentially death-invoking chemicals, permeated our surroundings. For the next six months, I deeply and joyfully inhaled it all.

Things were finally looking up. I rationalized that, with everything in our lives now going so well, surely Sean would be able to resist drugs and alcohol. He finally had a nice house, a good job and a loving partner. He couldn't possibly justify a relapse by taking his typical pity-me stance, right? Wrong!

With this mental foible came another lesson that I learned about alcoholics. Alcoholics drink when they are depressed, and they drink when they aren't depressed. Alcoholics just drink. That's what they do.

I deceived myself into believing that by creating a perfect life for Sean, I could help him overcome his addictions. How wrong I was! When a worm eats away at a perfectly good apple, you can remove the affected spot, but as long as the worm (alcohol) is there, the apple will become tainted again and again. The worm in this case was lying dormant, just waiting to rear its ugly head at the most vulnerable moment in our young lives.

Chapter 15: The Circle of Life

The act of dying is one of the acts of life.

Marcus Aurelius

As a youngster, I was fairly certain about two things: (1) somehow I would make my way to Colorado when I turned eighteen and (2) soon after my twenty-eighth birthday, I'd have a baby. Call it premonition or call it conviction; I just knew.

Sean and I had spent the last eight years together, and I desperately wanted to start a family. As soon as we stopped using birth control, I became pregnant. As I had predicted, the baby was due in April, one month after my twenty-eighth birthday. Once again, my life seemed to be on track. I was in control.

Four weeks later, however, I began to bleed. A white, mucous-like mass fell into the tissue on my hand. A sinking feeling came over me as a fog of disbelief enveloped me. I pondered, "Could I be holding my baby's embryo in the palm of my hand?" The minutes ticked by ever so slowly as I stood there, frozen, my eyes gradually filling with fluid sorrow. Not knowing what else to do, I reluctantly dropped the tissue into the toilet and painstakingly pushed the lever.

As I watched my baby swirl around in the bowl before plunging into the abyss, my life seemed surreal. "Why does everything have to be such a struggle?" I pleaded through intermittent sobs.

I hurried to the doctor, hopeful I was mistaken but apprehensive that I would hear what I already knew in my heart to be true. After a short exam, the verdict: I had indeed miscarried. My doctor assured me with a cold precision that I shouldn't be so distressed. "It wasn't really a baby anyway," he coolly remarked. He was right. It wasn't *a* baby. It was *my* baby. How dare he minimize my loss! I left feeling my life had betrayed me.

I drove home from the doctor's office that day, fighting back the salty tears rolling onto my lips, blinking repeatedly to clear my bleary-eyed vision so I wouldn't veer off the road. Sean met me at home later that afternoon. He too had been crying. We collapsed into each other to find comfort and strength.

Being a Jehovah's Witness and having a miscarriage taught me valuable lessons. Although we would like to think that we are masters of our own destiny, we aren't always able to fly in sync with the wind currents. Life's storms may thwart our **hopes** and **dreams**, even when we skillfully lay out a flight plan. Fortunately, it doesn't mean we have to cling weakly to a branch and feel sorry for ourselves, accepting our fate, playing the victim.

Everyone has a choice, every day. Every path we choose—whether we go right, left, straight ahead, backwards, or soar towards the heavens—leads us to a different destination. We can be defeated, or we can strengthen our wings and rally our inner strength to find a semblance of peace with the journey we are on, then set goals to alter our path. If we don't at least try to overcome the turbulence in our lives, we will be sucked deeply into the victim mentality vortex and perhaps never escape.

I wasn't about to let this miscarriage hamper my flight. Sean and I made love the next month and nothing happened. Disappointed but determined, we tried again. A few days later, I took a home pregnancy test. Unfortunately, it pronounced that I was *not* pregnant. But a little voice inside me raised doubts. That same day I made an appointment with a different ob-gyn. (I wouldn't go back to the first doctor because, quite frankly, he was an insensitive ass.) My trip to the doctor was filled with great anticipation. A movie billboard along the way said: "Parenthood, It Could Happen To You." That was a good sign.

The results came back: I *was* pregnant! This time I couldn't see the road as I drove home because the sun, which shone brightly in my eyes, created prisms through my tears of joy. Ahead the horizon glistened with the colors from a rainbow, and it was brilliant.

Unexpectedly, this day turned bittersweet. As I walked through the door of my lovely home, I noticed my answering machine blinking. I casually pressed the message button. It was my aunt: "Brenda, your grandmother has passed away." I dropped the prenatal information in my hands as I fell to my knees and wept. The woman whose hands I had held just a few months earlier, the woman who had lovingly hand-sewn a blanket for me with those hands, would never hold my child.

In the days that followed, I took solace in knowing that her quilt would someday wrap my child in warmth. Perhaps someday he would sense her presence watching over him. Ever since her departure, I have embraced the belief that my grandmother's spirit left this world—just as my son was conceived—so she could become his guardian angel. Later I will share a story that may challenge or quite possibly affirm your own beliefs.

**My last visit with my sweet grandmother
before she passed away at the age of 93.**

As expected, my mother did not attend her own mother's funeral because Jehovah's Witnesses prohibit their members from stepping into any "pagan" Christian church. How sad that the Witnesses' beliefs divided our family not only in life, but in death as well.

The next six months were magical bliss. I honestly doubt there has ever been a happier pregnant woman. I loved feeling a precious life grow inside me. Peace permeated my soul. I wanted and loved this baby with every ounce of my being. More than anything else, I wanted my child to have what I did not—a mother *and* father to unconditionally love and nurture him all his life, someone to help him move into adulthood as a happy, well-adjusted and independent person.

As early as my first trimester I anxiously collected baby clothes from thrift stores and garage sales and stuffed the spare closet with disposable diapers—forty-eight packs of them. I reasoned that if I invested materially as well as emotionally in my baby, I might not miscarry. Still, I continued to be very apprehensive when I didn't feel any movement for days.

During my last trimester, I coordinated a conference for my company involving over one hundred and fifty renowned scientists. As a result, my workload tripled overnight. But I was determined to show my employer that even a very pregnant woman could be a valuable, dependable employee. Two days before I went into labor, my supervisor noted that this farm girl was as strong as an ox and could probably be out plowing a field. Everyone saw me as a capable, diligent worker with an impeccable reputation. Unfortunately, all of that was about to change.

Chapter 16: The Snowman Puddle

It takes a lot of courage to release the familiar and seemingly secure, to embrace the new. But there is no real security in what is no longer meaningful. There is more security in the adventurous and exciting, for in movement there is life, and in change there is power.

Alan Cohen

After ten years Sean and I had succeeded in building nothing more than a dirty, lopsided snowman. So it didn't take much to melt our poor snowman of a relationship, reducing it—along with my failed **hopes** and **dreams**—to a sorry little puddle.

I wasn't sure if Sean's resentment of my success caused him to regress, but I knew it was over when he told me he had failed a drug test at work and was fired from his job for using cocaine. According to Sean, his employer said he'd be reinstated at work only if he agreed to check into a rehabilitation center. He insisted he was innocent and refused. When Sean's dad and I confronted him, he assured both of us that he wasn't using drugs again. Eventually

Sean's conscience got the best of him though because a few days later he admitted he had lied. Not only had he used drugs but he had started drinking again as well. What really shocked me was that Sean seemed more concerned about the validity of the drug test than he was about his unborn child's health or the fact that he had just deceived his wife and father.

I made a conscious decision, however, to let the issue slide because I was too concerned about our baby to slog through yet another all night "pity me" session. I certainly didn't want to have *another* miscarriage. I simply told Sean that if he didn't find a job and get his life together (i.e., give up drugs and alcohol) by the time our child was a year old, I'd ask him to move out. His response, uttered with an air of seeming indifference, was: "Fair enough."

Immediately my thoughts turned to our baby. If Sean had been using drugs when our child was conceived, perhaps something was terribly wrong. Is that why our baby seemed to kick so infrequently? I carried this anxiety with me for the next three months.

During my last trimester, Sean slept in every morning and barely lifted a finger to find a job while I dragged my big belly out of bed and put in a full day of work. He sunk into the throes of depression while my disrespect for him hit an all-time high.

One day I came home from work feeling so utterly exhausted and frustrated that I sat in my car and cried for nearly two solid hours. Not little tears—big tears—the kind of tears an old woman might cry from a lifetime of pain. For once in my life, I needed someone to be there to take care of *me*, to hold me and tell me things would be fine. Although there was another life growing inside me, I felt completely void. I had no empathetic husband to talk to, no devoted sister to confide in and no condescending mother to even say, "I told you so."

Granted, I had placed myself into a vulnerable position by becoming pregnant with an alcoholic. But there was no time for "what if's." After my sob fest ended, I realized that my child would be entirely dependent on me someday. I'd have to be up for the challenge. It was up to me to teach him how to not only fly, but soar. No one else was coming to rescue me. And no one else could help Sean, but Sean. With that revelation, I became emotionally liberated from the chains of an addict and fluttered nearly wingless into single parenthood.

Chapter 17: Life Begins Anew

It was the tiniest thing I ever decided to put my whole life into.

Terri Guillemets

In the Bible it says that after the Great Flood a rainbow shone forth as a sign to Noah and his family that the world should go on. Like that rainbow, when our son was born, I knew *my* world would go on.

Derek Stefan arrived in this world weighing in at eight pounds, four ounces. After the indescribable physical pain ceased, I found within the emotionally exhausted chambers of my heart the lasting love that I had been searching for my whole life.

Our child was blessed with lots of beautiful, thick, dark hair like my father, but his eyes were exactly like Sean's—squinty and narrow. Derek's other facial features, however, resembled me: chubby cheeks and round face. He was exquisite! Most importantly, he was healthy.

I would venture to say that the two most significant times in a woman's life are when she gets married and when she becomes a mother. Although I was hurt when my parents didn't attend my wedding, I could still empathize with my mother. I understood how she might feel uncomfortable with a Christian minister conducting the ceremony. Although, her religion would have permitted her to attend since the ceremony wasn't held in a church. But when neither of my parents showed up for Derek's birth, I developed a deep resentment. Here were two people who were present for the birth of *all* of my sister's children. (By now my sister had had two more children, a total of four boys.) We even drove to the hospital in the middle of the night to be with her while she was in labor! How my parents could show such blatant favoritism was beyond me. I knew that their absence had nothing to do with the geographical distance between us, their financial situation or busy schedule. It *did* have everything to do with the fear that Jehovah's Witnesses had instilled in my mother. She couldn't bring herself to visit her own grandchild because she'd have to be in my presence, in my home, and I was evil.

My family's absence at this significant time in my life picked a scab off a wound that had been healing ever so slowly. Regardless of the relationship they had with me, Derek was their grandchild. They owed it to him to welcome him into this world and into their hearts.

When I was a teen, my mother and father told me that after I became a mother myself, and only then, would I understand the sacrifices and selfless devotion they made for their children. They were right. With the birth of my son and all the maternal instincts welling up inside me, it became impossible for me to reconcile in my mind how my mother could abandon her own child. Where was her selfless devotion to *me*? Derek's birth really drove home the meaning of abandonment. At this milestone in my life, I embraced their words at a deeper level than even they themselves could ever comprehend. At a time when I needed my mother the most, she was nowhere to be found.

At first, Sean was very excited to be a father. He eagerly offered to give Derek his first bath. But after the novelty wore off, things changed. If Derek began to fuss, Sean became agitated and abruptly handed his tiny frame to me, wiping his brow afterwards, as if cradling his baby was more than he could handle. Derek sensed this in Sean and consequently he wailed every time Sean attempted to hold him. I wound up taking on one hundred percent of the responsibility for our child. Sometimes when I asked for help with Derek, *Sean* would throw tantrums. I felt like I was raising two children, not one. I knew in my heart that Derek would ultimately suffer if I stayed in a relationship with his father. *That* was the last thing I wanted.

When Sean wasn't working he spent his evenings in the dark, unfinished basement watching TV, smoking, and drinking on the sly. I frequently stumbled across haphazardly hidden beer bottles. This "cave" was indicative of Sean's emotional state—dark and cold. Even though I had struggled for nine years to get myself out of isolation, ironically I now found myself right back in it with Sean. Some evenings we barely spoke to each other. I frequently poked my head through the door at the top of the staircase and pleaded with him to come into our world and spend time with his son. I thought that if Sean bonded with Derek, perhaps he would ultimately choose us over his addictions. I knew my one-year deadline (to remedy his life) was approaching, and I **hoped** desperately that Sean would take the needed steps to save our family and, in the process, himself.

To the extent that Sean "checked out" of his parental role, I "checked in." I loved being a stay-at-home mom. Although I wanted to quit my job so *I* could raise Derek instead of a caregiver, I erroneously believed this wasn't possible. Since being fired, Sean had taken a substantial cut in pay with his new job, and we couldn't afford to lose my salary. I'd have to go back to work. What I couldn't have foreseen, however, was the struggle I'd face as the family's sole breadwinner. My father once described Hell as "what we live here on Earth." Little did I know it at the time, but I was about to live through it.

Chapter 18: Daycare Nightmare

If you happen to stumble across any news report that suggests we need better childcare in our country, I **hope** you'll believe every word of it and, if at all possible, find a way to make a difference in your community. I trust that this chapter will give you a little bit of insight into both the good and bad of what society calls child*care*.

My biggest hurdle by far as a new mother was finding a decent caregiver for my son. More brutally honest information—and less fluff—about what to expect would have been helpful. Few sources give you the specific tools, the do's and don'ts, necessary to understand what you are analyzing both from the perspective of a new parent as well as from the perspective of a caregiver. Such information is desperately needed.

Those first few, grand weeks with Derek disappeared in a blur. When Derek was less than one month old, I started investigating childcare options. Back then, very few licensed daycare centers enrolled babies. If you were lucky enough to find one, there was a waiting list a mile long because many providers were afraid to take a baby for fear of SIDS (Sudden Infant Death Syndrome). It was a rude awakening to learn that there was only *one* licensed daycare within fifteen miles of my home. When I visited, it reminded me of the third-world orphanages you see on TV with crying babies lined up in rows of cribs. The smell was questionable, the carpet was dirty and the room where they permitted the dozen or so toddlers to roam was unusually tiny and devoid of natural light. It reminded me of those windowless Kingdom Halls where I'd been trapped for hours. The caregivers did not seem very happy, although the woman who gave me the guided tour tried to put on an edgy smile for public relations purposes. Although the facility was convenient (right next to my office building), it just felt **wrong**. I knew in my heart that I wouldn't even leave a pit bull there, let alone my precious five-month-old baby.

Since we couldn't afford a professional nanny, that left us with just one other option. We'd have to hire a stranger to care for our son in our home. An ad in our local newspaper produced one response, an older lady named Cecile. A mother and grandmother herself, she seemed ideal. Again, I was about to learn that appearances could be deceiving.

One day I walked into my house to find Cecile sitting at the table feeding my six-month-old son corn chips and soda. Aghast, I explained to her that this was not a good nutritional choice and possibly a safety hazard—Derek could choke on the chips. I thought my point had been well received. I was obviously wrong. When I arrived home two days later, I found Cecile offering Derek hard candy. This time I firmly instructed her to follow my directions to the syllable, or else she'd be fired. Of course, I was torn. I didn't want to have to change caregivers after only a few weeks, especially since

Derek seemed to be bonding with her. I decided to give her one more chance. The neon writing on the wall became apparent, however, the moment she endangered my son's life and gave him an overdose of prescription medication. When confronted, she said, "I didn't think it was a big deal. I figured with twice the medicine he'd just get better faster." (Common sense is not so common.) After a frantic trip to the doctor, Derek was fine.

Pam, who was in her early twenties, was my second caregiver. She lived nearby in a mobile home park with her husband and one-month-old son. Our business arrangement seemed perfect because she could earn extra money and care for her own son simultaneously. Pam seemed very upbeat, fun and intelligent. I checked out her impeccable references and promptly hired her.

For a few days, things went as smooth as a baby's bottom, but when interviewed Pam had neglected to tell me that she had thyroid problems. She routinely bowed out of her daycare obligations to keep medical appointments. She continually assured me the next week's outcome would be different, so I hung in there with her. All told, I missed forty-eight hours of work in six weeks.

Understandably, my supervisor was developing terminal heartburn. His degree of agitation became evident when he suggested that I apply for another job within the company (a demotion). I knew he had no children of his own and couldn't possibly comprehend my ordeal. When I told him I couldn't afford to change jobs, he asked me to provide him with a written plan for getting to work 100% of the time. Unbelievably, he remarked, "Brenda, I want to be as important to you as your son is." I assured him I would get my personal schedule organized, but quite frankly, I was just stalling for time. I wasn't sure how I was going to resolve my problems. I felt trapped, at the whim and mercy of my childcare providers. After mulling it over for a few hours, the solution hit me. I needed a reliable backup, someone who could fill in at a moment's notice.

Jean, a congenial woman in her mid-50s, said she'd be willing to come to my home two days a week so that Pam could plan her doctor appointments for those days. By the second week, however, Jean pulled a "bait and switch." She asked if I'd bring Derek to her house instead; she wanted to start a daycare in her home. I visited her daycare and reluctantly agreed to her terms. Clearly our warm home was preferable to the unfinished, unwelcoming basement that housed her daycare center. Another concern was the concrete blocks that supported her makeshift toy shelves. I imagined a wobbly toddler stumbling and falling into one face-first. However, I knew I needed to go outside my comfort zone in order to ensure my continued employment. Now I was set. I had Plan B in place just in case Plan A fell through.

Plan A fell through like water seeping through my fingers, trickling away one drop at a time. It didn't happen all at once. In fact, by the time I got wind of what was happening, it was over.

Pam announced four weeks later that she was moving to Florida with her husband that weekend. While I understood her situation, I felt betrayed. She never had to face the pressure of leaving her baby with a stranger every day just so she could bring home a paycheck. She couldn't possibly appreciate the flack I caught at work in order to accommodate *her* schedule. Holding my anger at bay, I remained calm enough to talk her into giving me at least two days' notice. Since I had to find someone else immediately, the experts' advice ("carefully screen the childcare provider") became useless drivel.

That weekend (buckling my baby in and out of his car seat repeatedly until agitation produced screams from both of us), I posted dozens of ads in stores, laundromats and office buildings. Childcare provider number four, a nineteen-year-old, soon answered the call to take Pam's place. She lasted such a short time that frankly, I don't even remember her name. So for the purposes of this section, I'll call her "Sorry I'm Late Again." One of the points I drove home to Sorry I'm Late Again was that I needed someone I could count on. I explained my walking-on-eggshells situation at work and told her it was absolutely imperative that I get to work by 8 a.m. By the third day, Sorry I'm Late Again began showing up—you guessed it—late. I admonished her several times and docked her pay, hoping this would curtail her carefree attitude.

It was incredibly stressful to watch the clock tick by: 8:01, 8:12, 8:27 and realize how late I was going to be as I peered out the window, waiting for her to show up. How nerve-racking it was to have to race recklessly to work every morning, fearful of getting a speeding ticket, only to be met by glares from coworkers as I rushed to my desk in panic mode. Less than two weeks later, I cut my losses, fired her and went back to the drawing board.

Luckily, the relationship I had established with Jean paid off. She began caring for Derek full time after Sorry I'm Late Again departed. Although Jean was not licensed (taboo in the daycare world), she was a loving person and provided tolerable care for Derek. Jean gave us some stability...for a few weeks.

Suddenly, Jean announced that as a cancer survivor her health was declining. She'd have to stop caring for Derek. Jean's fight against cancer put my childcare problems into perspective. I felt incredibly grateful that Derek and I were at least physically healthy. (Little did I know that health problems would soon become an issue for us as well.)

Unbelievably, we had gone through *four* providers in only three months. This was *not* the kind of stability I wanted for my son. If this has been exhausting to read, imagine trying to live it! I harbored a bitter, hopeless feeling that I'd have to keep five people employed just to get to work 50% of the time. I knew I had to fight my rapidly developing victim mentality head on, lest it chisel me into an emotional invalid.

By now Derek was nine months old, full of energy and starting to walk. I had to consider a more reliable daycare situation. I was through conforming politely to other people's schedules. Again, I assumed that "licensed" meant better. I put my name on waiting lists with twenty-eight state-licensed, in-home childcare providers. None had an opening.

The local daycare center, which I will call SUX (so named to be phonetically appropriate), was the only other licensed daycare in my town. Unfortunately, they didn't take children less than a year old but would make an exception if the child could walk. Derek was able to cruise around a bit, so they agreed to enroll him once he reached eleven months.

Remember the post-traumatic stress I endured as a child after I forgot to feed my dogs? This anxiety resurfaced tenfold with Derek.

SUX, a well-known, accredited daycare center, was one of the most neglectful childcare environments I've ever seen. For those first few days, things seemed fine. But by the end of the first week, the true nature of the "care" Derek was receiving became brutally obvious. Every night when we got home, Derek proceeded directly to his highchair, whining and pulling on the tray, looking for any leftover food—ravenous. The minutes I spent trying to zap some food in the microwave stretched into an eternity, with him hanging onto my leg and wailing. Every night I felt like I was serving my heart up instead of chicken and veggies.

The daily reports that I received from SUX consistently stated that he ate "little to no lunch." When I questioned the staff, they nonchalantly remarked that he just didn't seem hungry. I suspected something more sinister was occurring, however, because Derek always had a healthy appetite. One day I pressed for the truth when talking to a substitute teacher. She confided that when it came time for lunch, Derek was falling asleep at the table. When that happened, the staff simply threw his lunch away. My baby was not being fed!

I stomped into the Director's office. I explained that Derek had been taking two naps a day before coming to SUX. Since he wasn't allowed to take his morning nap anymore (abiding by their rules) he was falling asleep at the table, right before they served lunch. Couldn't they just save his food and offer it to him again when he woke up? The Director told me my baby needed to follow their schedule and if he couldn't stay awake, that was his problem. My God! I had to get my baby out of this abomination they called child*care*. But where could I go? There were no openings.

Determined to improve the situation, I left messages for SUX's Regional Director. When I failed to receive any type of response from the regional office, I quickly surmised that one parent alone couldn't change corporate daycare culture. Yet, I knew it might be weeks before I found an alternate daycare. And if I pulled the plug on daycare, I'd have to quit my job. I was literally backed into a corner. The only solution in my mind was to leave work and feed Derek lunch myself, at least until I could get him out of there. The next day I left work at 10:30 a.m. with food in hand. When I arrived, the SUX director stopped me, saying it was against state regulations for any parent to bring in outside food. I was violating health regulations, rules that were in place for the well-being of the children.[9] I, however, failed to see how sending my child into a malnourished state on a daily basis in any way ensured his good health! I agreed to stop providing food if they would just

---

[9] I found out several months later that this wasn't true. In fact, in a lot of daycare homes and centers in Colorado, food is actually provided by the parents. The fact is, I was inconveniencing them with my daily presence, and they were fearful that any deviation from their rules would set a precedent with other parents.

allow me to bring in bottles every day. At least Derek would be getting some nutrition, something to fill his belly. Surely they wouldn't deny a baby his bottle, would they? (Derek had stopped using a bottle a month earlier, but I felt allowing him to regress was his only chance to survive there.)

A few days later I left work at 5 p.m. When I got to the daycare, everyone was outside on the playground. It was a scorching summer day, and I could hear Derek crying. Instinctively, my eyes honed in on his little form. He didn't see me because he was crawling on gravel towards a teacher who was about fifteen feet away. His shorts provided no protection against the jagged, hot rocks, and his knees were bloody and scraped. I watched in horror as a teacher "kneed" Derek off of her when he tried to grab onto the bottom of her pants to stand erect. (Remember, he was only eleven months old, and while he could walk, the unstable gravel was difficult for his little feet to negotiate.) Right then, I was faced with a dilemma. Should I go over to that daycare provider and beat the crap out of her, yelling obscenities for the entire city to hear (probably getting arrested in the process), or should I just race over to my crying son to embrace and comfort him? My maternal instincts took over and I went straight for Derek. "Please don't ignore his cries when he is crawling to you for help," I belted out. She countered with a smug look. "He needs to learn to walk outside and isn't going to get any special treatment!" My relationship with these teachers was comparable to walking on broken glass. I had to step lightly. I didn't want to make things worse for Derek by becoming a raving lunatic mother, even though that is precisely what substandard daycare was turning me into.

In what had become a daily ritual, I angrily stomped into the daycare center and switched the shoes on Derek's feet. All the adults there seemed to be dyslexic. Although I pleaded with them daily to make sure they put Derek's right shoe on his right foot—and the left shoe on the left foot—they turned a deaf ear. Now, if you think I was just being an overreactive mom, try walking around with *your* shoes on the wrong feet for just a few minutes and you'll understand the discomfort my baby was enduring for hours. What made this even more exasperating was that Derek had recently seen a podiatrist because his right foot turned inward when he walked. His one corrective shoe cost me over $50, and knowing that these incompetents were putting his shoes on backwards produced yet another anxiety in me—his feet could become further damaged.

With Derek's shoes properly situated, I gathered his scattered belongings. Upon opening the diaper bag, I found his two bottles completely full. I saw red! It was obvious to me that he was not only starving but possibly dehydrated as well. Immediately, Derek grabbed the orange juice bottle from my hand and began to chug it down as I collected the rest of his things. The fury with which he consumed the sustenance was more than his little belly could handle. Within seconds of gulping it down, he threw up.

When the daycare provider offered to help, I asked her why Derek had not received anything to drink during the day. She apologized and claimed it was an oversight. I asked, "What kind of care is this if my child has to make it through ten hours with no food or fluids?" She pointed out that he did have a hard pretzel at snack time. I angrily reminded her that he only had one tooth. How was he supposed to chew it? Her pathetic response (in the form of a nervous chuckle) was, "Well, he can lick the salt off." No comment has ever sickened me more!

It was agonizing to watch Derek's baby fat wither and give way to visible ribs, shoulder blades, and knobby knees. Yet, I knew I had to bring home a paycheck or we'd end up homeless, and *I* wouldn't be able to feed him either. There had to be a solution. I felt so guilty, as though I had abandoned my child, like my mother before me.

Remember the anxiety I felt sitting on that anthill in the Kingdom Hall? (To cope, I bit my nails until they bled.) Derek began manifesting his anxiety in a similar manner by sucking his thumb until it bled. Fortunately, through my own experience, I was able to recognize his plight. I didn't discount the thumbsucking as normal behavior.

I went home that night and filled Sean's ears with what Derek was going through—the starvation, dehydration, constant bloody diaper rashes from not being changed often enough and shoes on the wrong feet all the time. I showed him the red bite marks on his little arms inflicted weekly by the older toddlers. (In three months Derek had received eighteen such bites.) I begged Sean to quit his job and care for Derek while I worked full time. I knew we could make it on my salary alone. In my mind this was a viable solution. At that time, Sean was making as little as $150 a month. Derek's daycare alone cost $400. It didn't take a financial wizard to see that it wasn't cost-effective for Sean to work. Unfortunately, Sean didn't like that idea. Although he wouldn't give me a reason, it was my summation that Sean doubted whether he could handle the task. Admittedly, Sean's emotional state was fragile; it only took the slightest discomfort for him to begin drowning his woes in alcohol.

As quickly as those words left my mouth, I had an on-the-spot reality check: Would Derek be properly cared for by his own father—an addict? If Sean made a serious mistake with Derek, there would be no opportunity for a "re-do." (Sean's employer frequently made him "redo" his mechanic's work if a customer brought his car back and was dissatisfied.)

I quickly proposed that Sean begin working a second job so we could afford for me to stay home with Derek. Sean was less than enthusiastic; he felt he had such a long day already. *He* had a long day? As the sole responsible adult in our household, I begged to differ! Obviously, he was clueless.

It couldn't get any worse, could it? Yes, it could, and it did. Derek's exposure to so many ill children, combined with the fact that he was not being well nourished, left him vulnerable. He became a veritable Petrie dish of germs. As soon as one infection started to clear up, another one started. He battled high temperatures, coughing fits so violent that he threw up, and exhaustion. It was not unusual for us to make three trips to the doctor in one week.

With every illness Derek contracted, I cringed. If Derek got sick, I got sick. If Derek was sick, I couldn't take him to daycare. It was a vicious cycle—putting my child in daycare so I could work, only to have daycare infect him with everything known to science, which prevented me from going to work.

I tapped into my company's illness benefit only when Derek was sick so that I could minimize my time away from work. Even if I felt comatose, I always showed up for work, sometimes with a 102° fever. The pressure to be accountable to my employer felt like a vise squeezing my ailing body.

People tried to assure me, "Children just get sick a lot. It's normal. He'll soon build up some antibodies." I naively believed them. Yes, an occasional cold is normal. A sore throat now and again is normal. But no parent should have to sacrifice his or her child to an onslaught of germs—or inadequate, even abusive daycare—in order to bring home a paycheck and put food on the table!

Parents, or those with an elderly parent to care for, can relate to what I am about to describe: It's Tuesday, and for the last two nights you have been getting up sometimes four or five times a night to wipe away your ailing child's tears, offer medicine, refill the humidifier, make sure his blankets are on and ensure that he is still breathing. You hear every cough, gasp and whimper. At best, you know you will get maybe two or three hours of sleep that night. You think, "I'll be fine. I can sleep tomorrow night. Surely he will feel better then." You struggle through work the next day and fight to stay awake at the wheel of your car during the commute as your head bobs and your car weaves onto the shoulder of the road. It's now tomorrow night and the pattern repeats itself, but perhaps this time you don't sleep at all. The next night, it's the same story. It is finally the end of the week, and you realize you have barely slept two full nights over the last five days. Now, they say the Divine Being never gives you more than you can bear but you are beginning to have serious doubts. Just as exhaustion brings you to tears, your angelic child falls asleep in your arms. At last, you can surrender yourself to the sandman.

Now, imagine having an alcoholic spouse crawl into bed beside you about thirty minutes later, after having put away a twelve-pack of beer. You are finally in peaceful, heavenly slumberland when—ZZGGRAZZ!—he begins to snore so loudly that the rumbling jolts you awake. Irritation consumes every chasm of your soul. You know he only snores when he drinks excessively, which granted, is more often than not, but why of all nights does it have to be *tonight*! You nudge him and ask him to stop snoring but he doesn't hear you. You nudge him again, more forcefully. He finally stops. The anger consumes you and you struggle for the next twenty minutes to suppress your mounting rage. You try to block out the sickening stench of the booze that is lingering on his breath. Just as you start to drift off, his snoring hits another crescendo. You humbly admit defeat and angrily haul yourself out of your warm bed and into the cold night air. Meanwhile, hubby is oblivious; no, he is unconscious.

Needless to say, after several nights of tossing and turning, I started retiring directly to the guest bed. For the first time in my life, I understood how sleep deprivation, combined with illness, stress and constant physical overload could leave a person teetering on the brink of psychosis.

I know, I know! I should have remanded Sean to the spare room. But remember, I was an enabler. When you are living with an alcoholic, you tiptoe around their deplorable lifestyle so as not to upset them. You become stuck on a perpetual treadmill, trying to keep them happy so that *you* can have some peace.

Although I graciously (or foolishly) made this accommodation for Sean, I felt like a bad wife, sleeping in another room away from my husband, as my mother had done with my father. As a child, my parent's separate sleeping arrangements troubled me. I didn't want to be the wife who crawled into bed with her husband only to satisfy his sexual urges. I wanted more intimacy than that.

When I took the marriage vows, I never expected "for better or for worse" to mean that I would have to suffer at the hands of a self-abusive man. Somehow I foolishly assumed that self-abusive meant *unto yourself* and not *unto yourself and everyone else around you.* Such is life with an alcoholic. Yes, they hurt themselves. But in truth, they hurt those who love them every bit as much. The fact is, I don't think they ever truly comprehend the extent of the pain they inflict on others. In defense of his alcoholism, Sean used to say, "At least I'm not an abusive husband, Brenda!"

Although my days and nights were ravaging both my body and mind, I knew it was worse for Derek. He didn't have a voice, except through me. Determined, I scoured every source—referral services, newspapers, and acquaintances—to find a new, better daycare. While I spent the next two months desperately searching, I was forced to hand my innocent child over to SUX.

I wondered if anyone else had experienced the guilt I felt as a new mother for not being able to adequately take care of the child I had brought into this world. Had anyone ever felt the anger and betrayal I felt towards Sean for abandoning *both* his wife and child? I knew others were going through similar circumstances, but since I had no support system, it was hard to imagine that anyone could relate to my desperation.

"Well, Brenda, you know if you lived close by, we'd help you out," my father frequently commented. I knew he meant well, but his words stung. I couldn't live close by, and he knew that. If Mother and I had had a normal relationship, I'm sure she and my father would have stepped in until I was able to find a better solution. But that wasn't an option. Jehovah's Witnesses had erected a titanium barrier between us that was impenetrable. How nice it might have been to call up my mom and ask for help. How different life might have been for both of us if that "nice" Elder had never knocked on our farmhouse door.

If ever I was close to a nervous breakdown, this was it. Sitting on that anthill for nine years, and then sitting by Sean's side for another eleven years as he threatened to kill himself—none of that remotely compared to the torment I experienced for those few months as I watched my beloved child suffer neglect and malnourishment.

By the time I finally got my one-year-old baby out of SUX, his little body, usually cloaked in size eighteen-month clothing, dwindled to nine-month clothing. He had lost six pounds in three months—over one-fourth of his body weight!

What joyous relief it was when another local daycare facility said they'd have an opening in a few weeks. There was a light at the end of the tunnel—and it wasn't a train! Once the switch was made, Derek seemed more content, although he did continue to suck his thumb. While his residual anxiety troubled me, having to deal with a raw thumb—putting an antibiotic and a Band-Aid™ on it every night—seemed like a small trade-off to him starving.

Lisa and Michelle, the toddler-room teachers, seemed like patient, attentive souls to the frail little bodies left in their charge. While this daycare had some general problems (some days were better than others), the staff was willing to work with me and for the next two years this center allowed me to rebuild our lives and stabilize my career, which had seriously eroded away.

Derek was the joy in my life and brought incalculable smiles to my face. Somehow, during this wildly insane period in our lives, I managed to capture about two hours of his life on videotape every month, memorializing the precious time we spent together. Although our unadulterated quality time was limited (on weekdays we had as little as one waking hour together), it was indescribable. I'd blow onto his back and he'd laugh into his blanket, then yell "More, Mamma!" when I stopped. He'd crawl into my lap and play with my teeth while I pretended to nibble on his fingers and his belly laughter would sometimes bring me to tears. On the weekends, we'd visit the library to check out dozens of children's books. Every night, we'd cuddle in his bed and read until he fell asleep. If I lay on the floor, he'd crawl onto my back and draped his body over mine, resting his head on the back of my neck. We nearly became one (this union of ours continued for many years).

**Derek snuggles onto my back at the endearing age of
17 months and again at 6 years.**

My advice to new parents is this: Follow your gut and don't rationalize your concerns away, as I did. Closely examine the behavior of your child. If your little one looks lost and doesn't fit in; if the childcare provider doesn't help direct your child to an activity or take an interest in interacting with all the children, but rather just stands back and supervises; or if your child seems to only tolerate being there, a change is warranted.

A child should love or, at the minimum, look forward to going to daycare. If you find yourself constantly worrying about your child's care, racing away from work at the end of the day because you don't want your child to spend one minute longer there than necessary, something is *very* wrong. We need to stop making assumptions and start insisting on adequate care for our children. Remember: childcare providers work for us and *we have a right* to expect good care for our child(ren).

Bottom line: Either your child is already in good care, or he should be. It's that simple. Don't make excuses. Don't settle. Don't be afraid of change. Don't hesitate to drive long distances or out of your way. Your child is counting on you to protect him or her.

I want to end this rather serious chapter on a happy note by sharing a quick story. Lisa, one of Derek's daycare providers, was pregnant and Derek, quite curious, asked her why she had such a big belly. Lisa explained to him that there was a baby growing inside of her. After dinner that night, I stretched and said, "Ahhhhhh...My stomach's so, so full." Derek, quite puzzled, looked at me and inquired, "Mamma, you getting babies?" Needless to say, I almost fell over.

Chapter 19: Family Ties That Unravel

The family—that dear octopus from whose tentacles we never quite escape, nor, in our inmost hearts, ever quite wish to.

Dodie Smith

It has been said that the pessimist complains about the wind, the optimist hopes it will change, but the realist adjusts the sails. From the day I met Sean until the day I was divorced, I went full circle from pessimist, to optimist, to realist.

The deadline I had given Sean had slipped by virtually unnoticed because our daycare issues took so much of my attention. Still, I knew in my heart that my relationship with Sean was kaput. We had stopped making love nearly one year earlier, in part due to our separate sleeping arrangements. If he touched me or tried to initiate any warmth, I began to cry. I had lost all respect for this man and had nothing left to give. The demands of dealing with Sean's addictive lifestyle in addition to being a single (albeit married) mother had sucked me dry.

I took a serious look at divorce in the summer of 1991. While Sean was whitewater rafting, I felt a sense of relief to know he might die if the boat overturned. Even though I once loved this man and fought tirelessly to try to save him, this was all the clarity I needed to become a realist.

Sadly, we had failed in our relationship. Sean moved out in October of that year. Derek was sixteen months old.

Since I knew I could make the payments on the house, I gave Sean the last $1,000 from our savings account. I expected him to him move into an apartment but instead Sean lived in his truck, playing martyr. He was angry, and I don't blame him. He had lost so much—a precious child and loving wife; a beautiful new place to live; and the inherited and revered title of "father," something he would now have to actually work to earn.

I knew getting child support for Derek wasn't going to be easy. Sean refused to sign our separation agreement, knowing that doing so would make it difficult for me to pursue child support. Meanwhile, my incompetent attorney led me through a maze full of legal oversights and dead ends. For the next fourteen months, Sean didn't cough up a penny. Since Derek and I were accustomed to going it alone financially, I didn't fight this battle. But when the separation papers were finally filed, I made it a point to include one important stipulation: Sean was to never drink alcohol prior to or during his visitation with Derek. I knew that if he had so carelessly jeopardized my safety by driving drunk, then he'd have no qualms about doing the same with his son.

I also requested that Sean be given the majority of the visitation time—six days a week—because (1) I knew Sean would only use a fraction of this time, (2) I wanted to ensure that Sean could never cite limited visitation as the reason for his failure to be an involved father, and (3) Most of all, I truly wanted Sean to get his life together and be the father he needed to be for Derek.

Everything in my life at this point was spinning wildly like a top. My friend drew a cartoon (below) to help me realize that I wasn't always in control, nor should I expect to be. She also gave me a small stuffed doll. On it I wrote, "Brenda's voodoo doll" and proceeded to stick a pin in it. We had a running joke that some unidentified force was trying to ruin my life. The doll, perched on my windowsill for the next few years, served as a grim, yet humorous, reminder of my struggles.

Ugh! You mean this isn't "The World According To Brenda"

At times I wondered if Jehovah was punishing me for leaving the Witnesses. It was hard to shake their indoctrination. But then the rational part of my brain would chime in, "Don't be silly, Brenda. You just got involved with the wrong guy, that's all." I took solace in knowing that things would eventually get easier. Just like the clouds floating overhead, the only constant in life is change.

My relationship with Sean was usually peaceful if only for Derek's sake. In the years that followed, Sean drifted in and out of Derek's life. Sometimes he wouldn't see him for a year or more. For the longest time, I felt frustrated and powerless. I couldn't make Sean see that he needed to be a better father, but being the classic addict that he was, Sean blamed everything on me. Everything was about what was done *to* him, not what he was doing to create his own demise. But I knew I wasn't responsible for Sean's addictions (he started drinking at age twelve) any more than I was responsible for causing the rift in my family. In both instances it was I who sought to escape *their* dysfunction.

Unfortunately, trying to reason with Sean was a little like trying to use logic with my mother. The alcohol and drugs affected Sean's judgment the same way my mother's religion affected hers. Their only focus in life was their addiction.

I understood that Sean felt inadequate as a father; but it was Sean's responsibility, not Derek's, to build the bridge between them. As the saying goes, "Anyone can be a father, but it takes a man to be a daddy." Sean was now a father and he needed to take on the responsibilities that being a daddy entailed. But could he? Would he?

In the blink of an eye, three years had flown by since I gave birth and started my own family. It was 1993 and my dad had been nagging me incessantly to fly back to Pennsylvania with Derek. However, I hesitated and pondered his request with skepticism: Why should I spend my hard-earned vacation time and money to share space on this planet with a mother who'd just ignore me? My heart softened, though, when I realized that if I didn't go, Derek would lose the opportunity to create a memory of his grandparents.

Those who have lived in a tiny town know how quickly boredom can consume the leisurely minutes that tick-tick-

tick by. When I grew up, most of my entertainment was found outside: walking around in the woods, swinging from vines, picking flowers, and the like. But what do you do if you are in the country and it rains for seven consecutive days? Can you imagine being confined in someone else's house with a restless toddler? One might argue that at least we spent a lot of quality time with my parents, right? Well, not really. Remember, this is a Jehovah's Witness family.

The next morning as Mother was cooking pancakes, she looked over at my father, who was sitting right next to me at the breakfast table. As though I was nowhere in the room, she inquired, "Lewis, ask Brenda if she wants syrup on her pancakes." With great restraint, I tried to contain my amusement. After a moment of hesitation, my father began repeating her question for my benefit. I sensed that he saw the lunacy of our "communication." Before he could finish, I shot back, "Yes, syrup would be nice." Faced with this absurd verbal exchange, I could only chuckle (on the inside, of course). Then my mother did something most families would consider equally odd. She took her food and left the table. Why? Because Jehovah's Witnesses believe that they shouldn't eat with someone who has left God's organization. That hurt. Yes, even today Jehovah's Witnesses practice segregation. Rosa Parks would have been appalled!

Although my mother couldn't utter one syllable to me directly, she occasionally communicated through others: "Derek, if you had some nice clothes, I'd take you to the Kingdom Hall with me on Sunday." Somehow I squelched my knee-jerk reaction: "Over my post-Armageddon, rotting body you will!"

To my amazement, my mother attended an out-of-town religious assembly for most of our visit. She spent less than four hours with us that week. As usual, her need to immerse herself in her religion took precedence over anything else. When it was time for us to leave for the airport, she had the implausible audacity to ask my dad how soon I might be coming back with Derek because she didn't get to spend much time with him. Unbelievable!

After such an unpleasant visit, Derek and I returned to our *real* home in Colorado, and I vowed I'd never go back there again. If they wanted to see us, they'd have to take the next step.[10] After all, the road ran both ways between Pennsylvania and Colorado.

When I look back on our lives, I truly regret that my family missed out on getting to know Derek. They never experienced his first steps, first tooth, first word, first bike ride or first day of school. They never knew what it was like to watch him hunt Easter eggs and squeal with delight when he found one, proudly tie his shoes, or struggle to write his name. They never attended his school plays, brought him homemade soup when he was ill or watched him wildly tear open his Christmas presents after weeks of anticipation. Surely they must feel a void in their lives.

And what has Derek missed? What have the Jehovah's Witnesses stolen from him? He'll never know the joy of making cookies with Grandma, being spoiled on a shopping trip by Grandpa, or hearing stories of how Grandma and Grandpa met and fell in love. He'll never share an overnight visit with them, never frequent the homestead where his mother grew up and never come to know, never even meet, his cousins, uncle, or aunt. What a blessed, loving religion the Jehovah's Witnesses have found, indeed!

Once we got home, Derek continued to be sick in daycare. In less than three years, we made over *fifty* trips to the doctor. His illnesses were so frequent and so severe that I wondered if he had developed an immunity deficiency. Desperate to find an answer so I could help him stay well, I

---

[10] Since I left Pennsylvania twenty-five years ago, my mother has never come to Colorado to see us. To my father's credit, he has visited twice.

asked his doctor to do some tests. Even today I can hear his trembling voice and see his tearful expression as the needle pierced the flesh of his tiny arm. As I held him down while they drew his blood, Derek cried out, "Mommy, I...I don't want to do this any more!" Inside I was crying as loudly as he was. *I* didn't want to do this any more either! Something had to give. Our quality of life had become nil. Once more, I began a long, intense search for the right caregiver: someone who'd drive to our home, shower Derek with love and work for pennies.

At the height of all this chaos in our lives, Sean's mother telephoned and asked me to join them in an intervention on Sean's behalf. Sean had threatened suicide. But I had to draw the line. I knew that emotional taxation (i.e., being a single mom) plus no child support payments equaled one mother at her wit's end! I already had enough on my plate with sole responsibility for a toddler. Plus, my job was still in jeopardy due to all my absences. How could I possibly ask for *more* time off? By now, my heart was as hardened as a polished stone, because I had invested eleven years of my life failing to save Sean.

Rather than feel pity for Sean as the rest of his family seemed to be doing, I felt rage. In my opinion, no parent has the right to consider suicide. Once you bring a child into this world, you owe it to that child to be a living, breathing, involved parent. Parents who selfishly end their lives leave behind children who are forced to pick up the broken pieces. What parent has the right to leave their child dealing with such ongoing, permanent devastation?

I received a second call a few minutes later from Sean's girlfriend pleading for me to understand his situation (i.e., why he was nearly a year delinquent in child support). Less than two months after Sean moved out, he had latched onto an enabler, a caregiver, someone who needed to be in control and would deal with his flailing emotions (and finances) for him. As a result, Sean continued along in his role of helpless victim.

From that day forward I fought like a mouse struggling with a boa constrictor to get Sean to take *any* responsibility for Derek. While I couldn't force him to be an involved dad, I could at least insist through the court system that he help feed and clothe his son, i.e., make his child support payments. If I had to assume sole responsibility for all the discipline, sleepless nights, visits to the doctor, daycare worries, constant supervision, etc., the *least* Sean could do was write a check every month!

It may seem like I'm complaining about being a parent. I'm not. I love my son, and I don't regret anything I've ever done for him. Even as a teenager I knew that parenting would be a daunting task. Helping my sister care for my nephews gave me a little glimpse into my future. What I resented was that Sean and most of his family seemed to take the position that I alone should be responsible for Derek's welfare. Wrong! Our society, filled with deadbeat mothers and fathers, is indicative that this thinking is fairly commonplace. There is a wise, old adage: "It takes a community to raise a child." As a single mom, I truly understood the wisdom in this statement.

It was tough hearing my aunt talk continuously of God's goodness while she went on several expensive vacations. I was pretty much still in my atheist mindset at this point and even hearing the word,"God," sent chills down my spine. I couldn't help but wonder when it would be my turn. I held on to the belief that someday my ship would come in, and when it did, it was going to be a *yacht*, because I had been paying my dues for so, so long.

For almost three years I had been a single parent in every sense of the word. Exhausted, I needed some time to recuperate. One night I took a big leap of faith and told my aunt about the struggles we had endured, hoping she'd see my plight and come to the rescue. I asked if she'd look after Derek so I could get away and go camping overnight with my girlfriend. She graciously agreed. While I was thankful, I also had unspoken doubts that she would come through for me.

The night before we left, my aunt recanted her offer. She said her business got busy and didn't think it was a good time for her to leave. Oh, how I hated to be right about her! I felt horribly dismissed. Knowing the extent of my pain, how could she turn her back on me? The last few years had been a grueling marathon with no finish line in sight. I didn't just *want* to get away. I *needed* to get away.

Fortunately, Serpil, a Turkish woman who had been renting a room from me, overheard our conversation. She volunteered to step in as a substitute. While she was a lovely woman, I was afraid she would not be able to understand Derek and vice versa. (She had a pronounced accent.) Nevertheless, I took her up on her offer. I was truly desperate.

As my friend and I drove to the campsite, I experienced extreme anxiety. What if there was an emergency? Serpil wouldn't know how to handle the situation. She had no car and no way of getting Derek to a hospital if he became injured or developed a high fever. Even if she did manage to get him to a hospital, would Sean drive to the hospital to authorize treatment and comfort his son? As I reflected on Derek's tumultuous medical history, I became more and more anxious with every mile that rolled over on the odometer. Still, I was determined to try to enjoy myself, so I struggled throughout the day to calm my fears.

Unfortunately, Mr. Murphy's Law, with his twisted sense of humor, was about to strike again. (Keep in mind that Colorado is an arid state; it rarely rains.) Shortly after we had set up camp, a deluge flooded our tent. In the middle of the night, we hastily threw our wet, muddy sleeping bags and other gear into the jeep and drove the three hours back home.

My long-awaited respite turned into yet another frustrating, physically exhausting and emotionally draining ordeal. As soon as I got home, I broke down into sobs.[11]

Sometimes I felt like an eighty-year-old woman schlepping around a knapsack filled with years of worry. But Derek kept me going. A single hug from him made it all worthwhile. One day, in the wee hours of the morning, Derek crawled into my bed, snuggled close to me and whispered in my ear, "I love you, Mommy. You're the best Mommy in the whole world." I was half asleep. When I realized I wasn't dreaming, the words melted into my worn-out soul like butter on a hot frying skillet. I thought to myself, "How precious, innocent and loving. Derek is the best little boy any mother could have ever hoped for." When those words— "You're the best Mommy in the whole world"—echoed into my eardrums, my heart filled with joy and the heavy load I had been carrying lightened immensely. The captain, an adorable, blonde-haired, blue-eyed wonder, with his arms clamped lovingly around my neck, brought my boat, *a yacht*, into port. How in the world could I ever have missed it?

---

[11] In November 1997, I had a heart-to-heart talk with my aunt. Although she admitted that she had neglected our relationship, like Sean she made no attempt to invest in it. In June of 1998, I confronted her again. I told her I felt she was abandoning me, just as my mother had. My cousin suggested we seek out a professional counselor. While I was anxious to do so, my aunt refused. In November of 1998, I decided to let her finish her journey of separation from me and cut our family ties. I was, quite frankly, tired of hanging onto relatives who didn't want to be a stable part of my life.

Chapter 20: Preserving Derek

Bitter are the tears of a child: Sweeten them. Deep are the thoughts of a child: Quiet them. Sharp is the grief of a child: Take it from him. Soft is the heart of a child: Do not harden it.

Pamela Glenconner

When Derek's test results came back normal, my suspicions were confirmed. "Daycare-itis" was causing his deteriorating health. His immune system, although functioning properly, was unable to fight off the germ warfare being waged against him. Clearly, he was on the front lines and needed to be taken out of the war.

I promptly removed Derek from his daycare center and hired a twenty-one-year-old woman named Kim who turned out to be an absolute godsend. Amazingly, Derek stopped sucking his thumb after being home only three days. He had found peace.

Within the sanctuary of our home, Derek gained five pounds that first month and his personality blossomed. Over the next nine months, he was not sick at all, not even once. It wasn't exposure to all the germs that helped Derek build immunities and ultimately stay well as everyone promised.

Rather, it was the *lack of exposure* that healed him. He needed that break to rebuild and reenergize his disease-ridden body. When he got a cold nine months later, I didn't even flinch because it was finally "just a little cold."

After almost a year, Kim left to go work at a daycare center where she could make more money. If I had been wealthy, I would have doubled her salary to keep her. I naively believed that caring for Derek would be rewarding enough. But let's face it. If you're drastically underpaid (most childcare providers are) and the bills are piling up, you won't hang onto your job for long, no matter how many perks and thank-you's you receive.

With Kim's impending departure, I had to start looking for another daycare provider—pronto. I'd heard about a Montessori daycare home nearby. Montessori programs have an excellent reputation for teaching children through hands-on involvement, whole child development and positive role modeling. When I went to visit, though, I had some reservations. My JW indoctrination briefly kicked in. For years I'd been taught in the Watchtower organization that image is paramount. For example, a clean-cut, well-groomed person (JW) or well-maintained building (e.g., a Kingdom Hall) equated to "good." Anything less was "bad." Granted, the house was small and the grass was sparse. But then I remembered the middle school I attended in Pennsylvania. Although it wasn't exactly an Ivy League school and the playground was nothing more than a parking lot, the best years of my life were spent at that school. I made a conscious decision at that moment to look past the exterior (the house) and focus on the interior (the people). At that moment, I discarded my black and white JW perceptions about people and things.

After interviewing the caregivers, Karla and Becky, I felt at ease. They only had about four children in their care that day, but the kids all seemed very happy and mellow. They freely hugged Karla and Becky, both of whom hugged back. The atmosphere was peaceful and safe. They had a sandbox with all kinds of "diggers" (what Derek called front-end loaders) and dump trucks, and Derek took to it with a passion while we spoke. There was no state-of-the art jungle gym equipment, only an old swing and slide set. There were few toys but lots of learning materials: beads, blocks and books. After talking and observing for thirty minutes or so, I knew it was the nurturing environment Derek deserved.

Derek attended Becky and Karla's preschool for the next three years. He never cried when I dropped him off and was always happily engaged when I picked him up. I no longer felt the need to rush from work to save my child from a distressful situation. I knew he was content. Good child*care* did exist!

Becky and Karla did not just take care of the children. They also served as marvelous role models and inspired the kids' creativity. One day I arrived to pick up Derek and found him wrapped in aluminum foil and cardboard. He had wanted a suit of armor and Becky had lovingly helped him make one out of the materials she had on hand. He beamed, "Look mama, I am a shiny knight!" and it brought tears to my eyes. That was all I ever wanted—to be able to work and know he was happy. I knew they couldn't love him like I could, but I wasn't trying to compete with my daycare providers. I was, however, looking, for someone who could make my child feel special, accepted and secure. Becky and Karla provided that. Derek and I will forever remember them for the difference they made in *both* of our lives.[12]

---

[12] At one point, my neighbor inquired about my son's daycare situation. Of course, I raved about Karla and Becky. However, when my neighbor visited their daycare she looked at the exterior, not the interior, and commented that she couldn't leave her child in a home where there was a cobweb in the corner of the room. Granted, daycare is a personal choice, but I wish somehow my neighbor could have seen the daycare world through my eyes to realize that the only cobwebs present were the ones in her inexperienced mind.

By the time Derek was four years old, Sean was making an appearance about once a year. Although I wanted Sean to be a regular part of Derek's life, I must admit that I was somewhat relieved when I got a break from having to deal with his issues, his anger. Tranquility, something we hadn't known for a long, long time, knocked on our door. I suspect that the intervention launched by Sean's family helped him realize that he needed to make major changes in his life in order to become a healthy parent and involved father.

Still, people would reproach me, "A boy needs his father!" (as though it were *my* fault that his dad wasn't around). One day I ran across a brutally honest children's book, "Daddy, Daddy Be There," by Candy Dawson Boyd and Floyd Cooper. In a subsequent letter I sent to Sean, I tried to appeal to his paternal side. I implored, "Sean, you divorced me. You didn't divorce your son. Derek needs you! Please call or come see him any time." I then shared sections of this incredible children's book with Sean. Unfortunately, even its inspirational sentiments invoked no changes in Sean. How could it not?

Before Derek was conceived, one of Sean's favorite songs was Harry Chapin's "Cats in the Cradle," in which a father ignores his young son the whole time the child is growing up. Then when the father is older and wants his grown child to visit him, his son has the same myriad excuses as to why he can't find the time to visit his dad. Sean obviously learned nothing from the lyrics that had once touched him so deeply, because he was doing the same thing to Derek. I believe Sean identified so much with the song because he didn't feel like his father and/or mother had been there for him when he was younger. Now he was robotically repeating their parenting style.

Ironically, Sean saw Derek a mere ten minutes one year, yet he had no qualms about asking him to be in his wedding the following year. Derek was present for his dad's big day, but where had Sean been when Derek needed *him*? Where? I wish Sean's inexcusable behavior could be justified. Then perhaps all the children in this world with absentee fathers (or mothers) might never blame themselves for this void in their young lives.

Earlier that same year, Derek confided in me, "Mommy, I don't remember what my daddy looks like." I searched through our photo albums and handed Derek a photograph of the three of us from when Derek was just six months old. The photo had faded over time, just like his daddy. But the image couldn't replace Sean. And as hard as I tried, neither could I.

Chapter 21: Neon Signs

The truth is that our finest moments are most likely to occur when we are feeling deeply uncomfortable, unhappy, or unfulfilled. For it is only in such moments, propelled by our discomfort, that we are likely to step out of our ruts and start searching for different ways or truer answers.

M. Scott Peck

Miraculously, I was still employed, despite the fact that I had juggled full-time single parenthood with a full-time job. Still, I wasn't too confident that my services would be retained because my company was planning to terminate thirty percent of its workforce. Months earlier, a new Assistant Deputy Director had been hired. I'd been in corporate America long enough to understand office politics. Obviously, the company was grooming the Assistant Deputy Director to replace my boss. And if he left, I'd be next.

Rumors surfaced that a deal was about to be struck for employees as part of this arrangement. If I volunteered to leave, I'd receive a really nice severance; however, if I failed to volunteer and the powers that be decided to release the guillotine, I'd walk out with nothing but my head in my hand—and a pink slip. It didn't take a genius to know which route to choose. The problem is, I didn't have a clear direction. Where would I go? Could I even keep another job with all my childcare problems? Being a single mom made my dance with job insecurity seem even more awkward.

With just a few months to plan out my future before the blade dropped, I searched my heart and soul for answers. I was tired of working in a rat maze, never seeing daylight, dealing with obstinate coworkers, just pushing paper and whittling away the time I could have spent with Derek. Surely there had to be a way to put bread and jam (raspberry, of course) on the table that would be more rewarding. I desperately needed a sign.

My job wasn't the only thing I had to worry about. Now that Derek was five years old and about to start first grade, I knew scheduling dilemmas would soon shake up our world as well. The elementary school, which opened its doors at 8:30 a.m., was not conducive to my work hours. I didn't have any flexibility in my work schedule, especially given the amount of juggling I had been forced to do for so many years. My supervisor wanted me at work at 8 a.m. sharp. No excuses![13]

As much as Derek and I loved Becky and Karla, I knew we'd have to say good-bye to them. I needed someone who'd be able to transport Derek to/from school. Unfortunately, there was only one person who provided such a service. (Poor selection is one of the reasons people end up with inadequate childcare providers—providers are fully aware they have monopolized the service and simply don't care.) Sheba seemed very nice when I interviewed her. "I want the children to feel like this is their home," she warmly offered with a smile. Upon closer inspection, I noticed her house was clean and organized and the children were stoic, very much like the JW children I had seen at the

---

[13] Many schools today offer before and after school care, but at the time I needed it, it wasn't available.

Kingdom Halls. This seemed unusual for a "worldly," daycare environment, but I dismissed this big, red flag waving vigorously at me.

Derek was in Sheba's care for less than two weeks. During this time my usually happy and outgoing child became clingy and withdrawn. He'd hit me, something he had never done before, and cry when I left him with Sheba. I tried to rationalize his negative behavior by thinking, "This is just a transition. He misses Becky and Karla, that's all."

After only two weeks in Sheba's care, Derek had what I can only describe as a total meltdown. It was as though we were reliving his awful days at SUX but now he could verbalize his anguish: "Mommy, don't leave me here!" he pleaded. That morning, I promised Derek I'd call him as soon as I got to work. I felt torn. I wanted to stay and console my son, but I knew the office clock was ticking impatiently on the other side of town.

As soon as I got to my desk that morning, I anxiously pushed the buttons on my phone. When Sheba answered her phone, I could hear Derek in the background, still crying. When Derek came on the phone to talk to me, I could barely understand him. As soon as I asked why he was upset, Sheba interjected with: "Say good-bye. We have to go." Before I could utter a word, I heard Derek's crying escalate, followed by a dial tone. She had hung up on us! I burned hot— incensed. How dare she!

Without a moment's hesitation, I bolted out the door. When I arrived at Sheba's house, she was outside shoveling snow from her driveway. Her queer little smile reminded me of a child caught with her hand in the cookie jar. Derek, the only child in her care so far that day, stood meekly beside her, coatless and shivering. Although he was still weeping softly, his eyes lit up when he saw me. His relief became apparent when he opened his quivering mouth and sighed heavily. I grabbed his frosty hand, wiped his runny nose and started walking toward her front door. She asked what I was doing and I simply replied, "I'm getting his coat and he's going with me." I knew if we discussed the situation, our confrontation would escalate and frighten Derek even more. I didn't want him to see his emotional mother unravel and unleash her wrath on someone who desperately needed it.

Once we were in the car, Derek looked over at me and tried to smile as he brushed the tears from his cheeks. In a solemn, sheepish whisper he confirmed what I'd suspected: "She pulled the phone out of my hand and I couldn't hear you anymore." My heart sank. How unstable his world must have seemed to have his mother ripped away from him at the very moment he was seeking comfort.

As we drove to Becky's house, I assured him he'd never have to go back there again. Reeling with anger, I explained to Becky that I knew something had gone terribly wrong at Sheba's but that I wasn't sure what. Becky agreed to take Derek back until we found alternate care.

Later that evening, I went to Sheba's to gather the few things I had missed during our hasty exit. As we pulled into the driveway, Derek looked very concerned and warned, "Mommy, don't go in there. She might hurt you!" I assured him she wouldn't do any such thing. If anything, I wanted to hurt *her*! My son's desperate plea explained his demeanor over the last two weeks. Obviously, instead of caring for my son, Sheba had been terrorizing him.

It took a while for Derek to provide any details. If I asked him point-blank questions such as, "Why were you crying?" he would get very quiet and say he didn't want to talk about it. Over the course of the next few days, however, the physical and emotional abuse this woman tried to keep secret seeped through in normal, unrelated conversations.

Words alone cannot adequately describe my rage. It's a good thing Jehovah's Witnesses had instilled the commandment, "Thou Shall Not Kill" into my vocabulary!

However, I was hardly willing to "turn the other cheek," as Mother had done when my teacher abused me.

I reported this so-called child*care* provider—who purported to want children to feel like her home was theirs, heaven forbid!—to the childcare licensing authorities. Once they were done questioning Derek, they went to Sheba's home to interview the other children. It wasn't a surprise when I learned that the children offered nothing to substantiate Derek's allegations. After all, how many adults, let alone children, would be willing to speak the truth with their abuser sitting right there glaring at them? The social worker did just enough to file a report but not enough to ensure the truth was revealed. She concluded Derek was able to verbalize his abuse. But it was Derek's word against Sheba's; since Derek was merely a child, Sheba was exonerated.

In addition, the court system allowed Sheba to keep several hundred dollars of prepaid childcare in lieu of me providing her with two weeks' termination notice, per her contract. But there was no way I was going to send my son back to her under those abusive circumstances to "get my money's worth." In my mind, the legal system failed us.

It took at least six months for Derek to heal from the trauma he endured those brief two weeks, and even longer for me. Despite the disappointing outcome, I was proud that I had taken a stand on my child's behalf.

Enough was enough. My struggles with childcare through the years helped me define the path I needed to walk following my company's layoffs. *I* would become a childcare provider, but not just a mediocre one—a great one! I was about to put the *care* back in childcare. My son and others like him were finally going to get the nurturing they needed and deserved, and Queen Sheba was about to get a run for her money!

My father's belief that "Hell is what we live here on Earth" did, unfortunately, ring true for us with our nightmarish daycare experiences. However, Hell was about to freeze over and we were about to experience something a little more heavenly, something angelic, something truly remarkable.

Chapter 22: Guardian Angels

If I have freedom in my love, and in my soul am free.
Angels alone that soar above, enjoy such liberty.

Richard Lovelace

In 1996 my dad uttered the words I had been expecting to hear for over twenty years: "Jon has been disfellowshipped." After watching my nephew endure years of beatings, I wasn't surprised. While I'm sure this announcement devastated my sister and her family, I saw it as a golden opportunity for me to reconnect with a long-lost family member.

Jon, now legally an adult at age twenty-one, was working as a cook in a local restaurant in Pennsylvania. After I researched the restaurant's phone number, I apprehensively punched the keypad on my phone and took a deep breath. Jon wasn't working that night, so I fumbled to leave a message with his supervisor—a message long enough so that Jon would know who I was but one short enough that I wouldn't appear too emotional or anxious. For the next week, I waited impatiently and rehearsed in my mind what I might say. What do you say to family you haven't spoken to in over seventeen years? Would Jon even return my call?

Every time the phone rang, my hands trembled as I pressed the receiver to my ear. Usually it was a solicitor or one of my friends calling just to say hello. Then one day I heard a voice that seemed somehow familiar, but much deeper in tone than the four-year-old boy I had left behind. It was my sweet nephew. It was Jon!

This young man on the other end of the phone line seemed nervous, even more so than me, but also fearful that his mother might learn of our conversation.[14] We made small talk before I eased into my perception of this so-called "Truth" that he had been raised in. I wanted him to hear my pain so he could feel safe in revealing his own. I shared with him how as a toddler he had been my shadow, following me literally everywhere. As he spoke, Jon sounded like a lost soul with no direction. He said he remembered little about his early childhood but did recall my kindness. He knew how much I loved him. Through the years he often reflected on his life while staring at my graduation picture, which had been lovingly displayed over the fireplace in my parents' home for over twenty years. I asked him if he needed any money to help with his new apartment. He said he was fine. Based on my own experiences and how difficult my life had been after emerging from the cocoon, "fine" didn't convince me. I concluded our hour-long conversation with a genuine plea: "Call me if you ever need *anything*."

About a week later, Jon contacted me again. He needed money. I didn't even ask what he intended to use it for because I wanted to show him that I trusted and supported him. The next day, I dropped $200 into the mail. I felt like Jon's living guardian angel, much like my aunt who had been sent to my home twenty-five years earlier to help me. History did seem to be repeating itself. Unbeknownst to me, this

---

[14] JWs induce fear and paranoia into their members. If you even talk to anyone who has been disfellowshipped, you too can be excommunicated and forever shunned by your family..

would be the first and last time we would communicate as adults. Jon's life was about to take a very different path from mine.

Jon used my hard-earned money to purchase alcohol and host a party for his friends. Afterwards, while intoxicated, he wrapped his car around a tree and broke his neck. He was expected to recover, but for the next six months he'd have to wear a halo drilled into his skull. While I was relieved to hear that he hadn't been more seriously hurt, I was extremely disappointed that he had made such a reckless choice.

Jon moved back into my sister's home as she had hoped—defeated. Now his Jehovah's Witness parents could help care for his medical needs and "provide loving assistance." A few months later, Jon was reinstated as a member of their church.[15]

While Jon may have been wearing a literal halo to support his broken body, I learned rather abruptly that he was no "angel." A few years later, however, I was introduced to a real one.

I had tagged along with my son's class on their third-grade field trip. Derek and I eagerly anticipated our first school excursion together. We really looked forward to enjoying the crisp mountain air and the opportunity to interact with the other parents and children. As night rolled around, we began laying out our sleeping bags in the corner of the lodge close to the others in our community. It was five minutes until lights out. As I sat on my sleeping bag with Derek right beside me, a lightning bolt of intense panic hit me. "Can't breathe. No air!" Someone was telling me we

---

[15] Unfortunately, Jon did not have the common sense to use a rare opportunity to establish independence as I had done. I wish him well but can't help but wonder how his conscience copes with the fact that he betrayed my good faith in him. Where was the morality the Witnesses claimed to have instilled? Today Jon is "disassociated" and his grandparents, parents and siblings have little to do with him.

weren't safe. I tried to dismiss the feeling, but it was too powerful. Grabbing the sleeping bags with one hand and Derek with the other, I announced that we were going to sleep in the basement. Everyone thought I was crazy, including Derek, but he didn't question my authority.

After we awoke the next morning, we climbed lazily to the top of the staircase, only to discover several people in a semi-conscious state. Carbon monoxide had inaudibly curled its way through the main level and poisoned the unsuspecting sleepers. As we evacuated the sick and opened the windows, a stream of ambulances arrived to take approximately thirty people to the emergency room. We stood outside for three hours in a snowstorm while the fire department evaluated the building's safety. Needless to say, the trip was cancelled. We went home hungry and cold but very thankful that we awoke before anyone died.

The very next year, Derek's school planned another field trip. I received another unexpected message: "You *must* go." However, I knew that, after the last fiasco and subsequent outrage, parents weren't invited. I resigned myself to defeat and tried to reassure myself that everything would be fine. A few days later I got a call from the school. The staff had decided to enlist a couple of parent volunteers. Since I was one of the few who didn't get sick or complain last time, they thought I might be a willing candidate. Would I like to go? Would *I* like to go? Of course! While I wouldn't be able to sleep in the same tent as Derek (a father would sleep with the boys), I felt reassurance that I would at least be close by.

The first night came and went without incident. I began to dismiss my sixth sense as just a nervous mother's separation anxiety predicated by a previous bad experience.

During the second night, however, things changed dramatically. A tornado ripped through the area. Our campsite was located in the boonies, set more than twenty-five miles back on a secluded dirt road. Night had already fallen so it was very difficult to see. The children's terror climaxed as we haphazardly threw our belongings into the cars. The winds continued to whip ferociously. As the storm grew closer, my tent was literally ripped out of my hands, never to be recovered. We piled the kids into cars any way that we could manage—on top of clothing, sleeping bags and each other. Pandemonium reigned as we drove to a 4-H emergency shelter. The children who didn't have parents with them were the most upset, visibly shaking and crying. As I held Derek in my arms and assured him that everything would be fine, I knew why I was there—to protect and comfort my child and as many others as I could.

Although we were forced to sleep on a cold concrete floor that evening, we were safely out of the path of danger. The school learned its lesson: future field trips were cancelled.

What makes these experiences quite unusual to me is that, at the time, I considered myself an atheist, devoid of any real spirituality in my life. Living as a Jehovah's Witness for so many years stripped away any notion that there is life beyond this one. One could understand a religious person having such an experience and could chalk it up to the fact that he or she is probably just embellishing his or her current belief system a little. But when this happened to me, it opened my eyes and heart. Since that moment, I have come to believe that somehow my grandmother communicated with me. We must have guardian angels looking after us. There is no viable explanation as to why I would look around the room at the last minute and think, "Can't breathe. No air!" In my mind, the correlation ties too closely to carbon monoxide poisoning for this to be a mere coincidence.

When I was a young girl, my father shared with me a supernatural experience he had had as a youngster. It still sends shivers down my spine when I think about it.

According to Dad-i-o (what I fondly called my father as a child), his similar encounter went something like this: As a

wee lad in elementary school, he walked *ten* miles from the
bus stop to his house every day. OK, he was exaggerating. It
was really more like *two* miles! One day after school as he
reached the crest of the hill, he gazed upon a landscape that
appeared quite different from the one he had seen that
morning. "Where's my house?" he asked his friend. As he
walked closer, he realized there had been a fire and that his
house had burned down. Tragically, his baby brother died,
and his mother was badly burned trying to save him.

The previous evening an invisible entity had paid a visit to
their home. It was bitterly cold with a steady snowfall.
Nevertheless, all through the night, his entire family heard
loud knocking around the perimeter of their home. Curious,
they looked outside, but found no one there. They also
noticed that there were no footprints in the snow that might
have given away any neighborhood pranksters. The knocking
continued for hours, making my grandfather very angry. At
some point after my father left for school the next morning,
the house caught fire. My father adamantly believes to this
day that someone was trying to warn them that danger was
imminent. In light of my own encounters, I can't help but
agree. I often wonder who their guardian angel was. If only
someone in his family had taken heed as I did.

I believe that my son's strong sense of self and balanced
outlook come from more than his inherent common sense
and a mom who is a good mentor. I believe that his great-
grandmother is contributing as well. Perhaps that quilt that
she made so lovingly for me, the one that embraced me at the
vulnerable age of eighteen as I exited from my cocoon, and
which now envelops Derek, links her world to ours. It may be
that her spirit—a spirit that gives us the wisdom of a much
older, wiser woman—is woven into that special blanket.

Chapter 23: Peace of Mind Childcare

> *Success, happiness, peace of mind and fulfillment—the most priceless of human treasures—are available to all among us, without exception, who make things happen— who make "good" things happen—in the world around them.*
>
> Joe Klock

In January of 1996, I volunteered for my company's layoff and received a $25,000 severance. Uncle Sam "generously" left me $15,000. I took that money, purchased a pre-owned, forest-green minivan (so I could haul all those children around) and turned my basement into a colorful, child-safe playroom. I also spent in excess of $800 on various state-mandated modifications to my home.[16] CPR, first-aid and child development classes cost another $200. The timing for

---

[16] The most outrageous modification involved me raising the grass near my back deck *1 inch* in order to meet a 12-inch-or-less deck-to-grass guideline. I half-seriously, half-jokingly informed the licensing worker that if she'd just wait until spring, the grass would grow. I still laugh about the absurdity of their rule, especially after they so easily dismissed Derek's abuse the year before.

the layoff couldn't have been better. The resulting financial windfall set my new business in well-oiled motion.

By the end of the month, I had five children enrolled. I called my new venture "Peace of Mind Childcare." It was a fitting tribute to what I had hoped to find in SUX and Sheba. I wanted to be more than an indifferent babysitter like them; I wanted my home to be a learning environment. So I purchased preschool materials and taught the youngsters how to count, read and write. We devoured multiple books every day and went on educational field trips every week. The children were like sponges, absorbing everything.

Although I participated in the state's food program, I encouraged parents to provide supplemental food so that if their child fell asleep before lunch, I could reheat their food and serve it to him after he awoke. I provided a daily typewritten report to parents, detailing what we had done, what the children had learned, the titles of the books we had read. Then I added handwritten personal comments such as when they had their diapers changed, funny remarks they had made, what their general mood was on a particular day and what they ate. I didn't just say "Tommy ate well." I wrote down specifics: "Tommy had four tator tots, five chicken nuggets, a few slices of peaches, and milk for lunch." Keeping this level of detail forced me to pay attention to the children's needs and not become complacent.

One day a mother knocked on my door and asked to interview me. She anxiously shared that her one-year-old child had failed to gain weight in his previous daycare. I wondered if he, like my son, had sucked salt from pretzels while in daycare. The doctor advised the boy's parents to get the child to eat more, but had no medical explanation as to why he was behaving this way.[17] I could see the little boy's

---

[17] I now know that this woman came into my life to help me somehow right the injustice that Derek had suffered while being starved years earlier at SUX.

resistance to food and how much he loathed being confined. I could relate to his feelings, having spent years in confinement in the Kingdom Hall. He simply hated sitting still and didn't feel the hunger pains that most kids felt. Unlike SUX, I began paying special attention to this child's cues.

Within a week, he was sitting with the rest of the children (during the entire lunch period) and demonstrating a healthy appetite. By the end of the month, he had gained almost three pounds. His ribs no longer protruded. His mother sang praises to me with tears in her eyes. It felt so good to know I had treated this child as an individual, not as one of the herd.

I have always considered myself an excellent parent, extremely patient and loving. When Derek was very young, I had the great fortune of discovering Dorothy Law Nolte's book entitled, "Children Learn What They Live." Dorothy wrote this at a time (1954) when parents expected children to do as they were told without reservation. When I read her book, it validated my parenting skills, for I had been instinctively raising my son according to her principals. I posted the poem from her book on the playroom wall for all my daycare parents to see. What a better place the world would be if every teacher, parent and childcare provider applied Dorothy's incredible words of wisdom!

I loved and treasured my daycare kids. I understood the impact my care would have on their precious young lives. Day in and day out I treated my charges according to Dorothy's guidelines, observing firsthand the positive results it had on them. I have never had such a rewarding—nor challenging— job.

I admit it; I wasn't perfect. Providing childcare services stretched my problem-solving skills and instilled a level of patience in me far greater than I ever knew was possible. Parents would often say, "I don't know how you do it—so many young children at once." I wondered myself some days!

When we went out in public, the usual inquiry was, "Are these all yours?" That one always made me laugh—and cringe. Parenting just one small child can be incredibly challenging, but *eight* of them? Well, that's a downright daunting task. And the twelve- to sixteen-hour days didn't help.

Caring for so many young children wore me down emotionally, physically and mentally. Did you know that the average four-year-old asks one hundred and thirty-seven questions a day? Granted, most of their questions aren't difficult, such as: "When do we eat?" or "Where is my crayon?" or "Can you tie my shoe?" What is so difficult is hearing the same questions over and over again, day in and day out. If you multiply all those questions by six children, you will understand why, on some days, I felt like my brain had been scrambled into an omelet!

But the hardest thing by far was the illness that gripped our lives yet again. Anyone who works with daycare children can attest to one fact: daycare kids' colds are not simply colds. Young children breed germs unknown to modern medicine (the germs then mutate mercilessly). They don't have a case of the sniffles. They have Godzilla-like respiratory infections that would level Tokyo!

During the previous years, Derek and I had been nearly free of "daycare-itis." As soon as I started taking in very young children, however, the bouts of colds, flu, croup, pink eye, and the rest plagued us once again. No matter how much I disinfected the house and toys or washed the children's hands, we were continuously sick. (Clearly, I had done the right thing by removing Derek from daycare for one year after he turned three. Otherwise, he may have never experienced good health during his first six years of life.)

While germs wreaked havoc on our bodies, the preschoolers wreaked havoc on our property. I threw out at least $1,000 in broken toys every single year. Wear and tear perfectly describes daycare life. It is a subtle, almost invisible, but slow, methodical death to everything a child has access to, which is pretty everything that isn't locked up.

One of the things I learned from running my own childcare business was that most parents tend to seek out larger daycare centers because they foolishly believe (as I once had) that they are somehow better. In reality, SUX didn't remotely compare to the quality of care I provided.

For the first time, at the age of thirty-five, I developed allergies and other physical problems that included severe and constant lower back pain, unusual temperature fluctuations, night sweats, and general agitation and depression. I spent a fortune on yoga, acupuncture, physical therapy, shoe inserts, Echinacea, special pillows, massage therapy and various specialists (including chiropractors and homeopaths). No one could help me. I felt emotionally and financially spent. But, no one had to beat me over the head with a 2x4 for me to realize what was happening: my body was deteriorating from so many years of illness and stress.

After two years of poor health, I learned that I was perimenopausal (in the beginning stages of menopause). Within two more years—by the age of 39—I was post-menopausal, completely through menopause. When I asked my doctor what could cause a woman of my age to go through such a thing so early in life, she replied, "Well, have you experienced any excessive stress?" I humorously pondered: "Hmmm, which stress?"

- Stress from struggling to survive for nine years while tied to the Jehovah's Witnesses' anthill?

- Stress from knowing that my own flesh-and-blood mother, brother and sister had disowned me?

- Stress from living in turmoil for over a decade with a suicidal addict?

- Stress from coping with the demands of full-time single parenthood and a full-time job?

- Stress from feeling utterly helpless as a mother—that I couldn't even rescue my own son from abuse and neglect?

- Stress from dealing with countless sleepless nights, my body riddled with bacterial and viral infections?

- Or was it the stress from having eight children in tow fifteen hours a day, combined with the fact that I hadn't dated for almost eight years? Perhaps my body, after enduring eight years of celibacy, took a peculiar stance of its own: "This woman is obviously abstaining from sex for a reason. Can't you see she has eight kids? Emergency! Emergency! For goodness sakes, let's shut this woman's reproductive system down now."

OK, I'm laughing now. But at the time, it wasn't in the least bit funny.

Regardless of which stress(es) were responsible for crippling my body, I realized I had to stop sacrificing myself in a quest to care for others before I experienced a catastrophic meltdown. Over the course of the following year, I transformed many aspects of my life and home so I could begin to care exclusively for older, school-age children. The benefits came immediately: fewer illnesses, less stress and limited destruction of personal property.

The change was long overdue for Derek as well; he needed to be around children his own age. We all relished the field trips, more complex crafts, birthday parties and more meaningful friendships. When given the opportunity to stay home (many of the kids were old enough to legally stay home alone), the kids usually pleaded with their parents to come to my house. They enjoyed it that much. In some ways, caring for these preteens and sharing stories with the girls helped me understand more fully, and helped me recapture, what I had missed at that age.

Even in the most stressful of circumstances, providing childcare for so many other children seemed like a cakewalk compared to having Derek in substandard daycare. My most immediate reward was the realization that I had become even more of an influence in my son's impressionable young life. I got to see his world through his eyes by living in it with him every day. I cherished this time with Derek and if I could do it over again, I would. I have no regrets.

One thing is clear, as a child*care* provider I made a significant impact on a lot of young people's lives. Like my role models Becky and Karla, I gave out hugs and praise constantly and focused on the positive. I was more than a babysitter. I provided peace of mind to dozens of parents and their remarkable little ones.

What would I have changed? I would have freed my son from his daycare nightmare sooner by freeing *myself* from the chains of corporate America. Unfortunately, sometimes you must experience hardship to become a little wiser.

Chapter 24: Forgiving, Making Peace, Moving On

Forgiveness is a rebirth of hope, a reorganization of thought, and a reconstruction of dreams. Once forgiving begins, dreams can be rebuilt. When forgiving is complete, meaning has been extracted from the worst of experiences and used to create a new set of moral rules and a new interpretation of life's events.

Beverly Flanigan

When the Watchtower organization and "The Friends" (i.e., JWs) held me hostage, I experienced firsthand how they successfully control people through fear. Many want-to-be deserters silence any thought of departure, fearful of the dangers that lurk in the outside world, fearful of the repercussions from the Elders, fearful of living a life without their family's approval. Not only are they incapable of thinking for themselves, they are forbidden—and terrified—to do so! They do not allow anything into their life that challenges their religious philosophy. They are never allowed to venture out of their cocoon. They are never, ever free.

Because I am able to understand this, I no longer hold any animosity towards my mother for what the Watchtower organization has done to our family. I know that she is as much an insect caught in their web of lies as I was. She believes she is doing the right thing and is committed to saving us all—you and me. This is her version of love, even though I don't feel that love.

Even still, every day I am faced with the knowledge that I will never send my mother a Mother's Day card, invite her to dinner or talk with her on the phone. I will never embrace her again or hear her say, "I love you, Brenda." If my mother had physically died the day those nice Jehovah's Witnesses knocked on our door, the raw grief would have eventually subsided and would have given way to precious memories. But this is not the case because my mother died a symbolic death instead. She is within reach, yet untouchable. There is no closure. I cope with this oxymoron by reminding myself that when something is out of my control, *acceptance is liberating.*

If I had not known my mother before she was caught in the web of the Jehovah's Witnesses, if I had not presented flowers to see her smile, if I had not felt her embrace as a young child, if I had not tasted all those homemade meals and enjoyed those playful moments with my cousins, would I feel the same sense of loss I feel today? I don't believe I would. You can't truly miss what you have never experienced.

This insight helped me make the decision to divorce Derek's father when Derek was very young, *before* Derek ever bonded with him, and before he had a chance to see us together. Was it the right choice? Yes, I think so. Because Derek has never known anything but life with his single mom, he doesn't seem to miss having his father around. And yet, I do believe that someday Derek will look back at his life, as I have and perhaps wonder, "Why?" *Why didn't my father come to see me more often? Why didn't he ever call me, just to talk? Why didn't he make me more of a priority in his life?* And when that time comes, I **hope** he will take solace in knowing that who he is today was molded from his life's experiences yesterday. To wish for a different past would be to wish for someone other than who he is. I **hope** he will forgive his father, make peace, and move on, just as I have done.

I **hope** Derek will learn that acceptance is liberating.

Derek's conflicting feelings about his father were evident in a poem he wrote for me on Mother's Day in 2001. He was just ten years old, the same age as me when my world was turned upside down. His thoughts are proudly displayed in a frame on my bedroom dresser, handwritten on college-ruled notebook paper, wrinkled by a little boy's intensity and spoken from the heart. I will treasure it always:

Momo, Momo, you are really cool
But that dad jerk, he's just a mule
So I'm writing a poem for a special mom on her day off
So with a wiggle of the toes and a spray of the hose
Hope this works cause here it goes

Mom, a mom is more than just there
She is not just like your underwear
For if a mom worked up a cough
She would have to work on her day off

So I say today you should sit on your bruised butt [18]
I'll do what I can to make your day pure bliss
But you got to let me have some freedom miss!

I say again a world without moms would be a disaster
So I should write this poem faster
Well toot-a-loo, I hope I made my point clear
So with a twist of the ear,
I wish you Happy Mom's Day

---

[18] Derek is making a reference here to me sitting on my "bruised butt" because I had just fallen the day before and landed painfully on my backside. It was not an attempt on his part to be disrespectful.

Oh, how I wish I could have been inspired to write something similar for my mother when I was ten, instead of the "All Alone in the World" story. I wish I could have said, "I love you," somehow.

Now, thirty-some years later I can.

I love you, Mommy.

Chapter 25: Finding Meaning in My Suffering—A Revelation

When I can look life in the eyes, grown calm and very coldly wise, life will have given me the truth, and taken in exchange – my youth.

Sara Teasdale

Something unexpected happened while I was writing this book. Like a butterfly trapped in a cocoon, this book also experienced a metamorphosis. Initially I began writing my memoir as a legacy for my son, but I quickly learned that it needed to take on a much broader agenda. This revelation occurred in October of 2004, twenty-five years after I left the Jehovah's Witnesses. I began an internet search for former members through a website, www.meetup.com. The Denver, Colorado, group needed an organizer for their meetings so I apprehensively volunteered. There, for the first time, I met an ex-Witness—someone like me. Three months later I was inspired to create a newsletter, "Cocoon." Since then, it has become a support vehicle to help thousands of ex-JWs and former cult members worldwide.

While completing my book at the same time, I discovered that there are parallels to be drawn between one generation and the next, parallels that bind us to our ancestors and which serve as a road map to our children's future. What parallels exist in my life? There are many, but I will share what I believe to be the most obvious and significant.

Parallel #1—Abandonment

My mother's abandonment of me and Sean's estrangement from Derek. Derek and I have both, in a sense, lost a *living* parent.

The good news is this: No child has to have two perfect parents in their life to become a whole, healthy person. Beaver Cleaver and his TV family are simply a fantasy created by dreamers in Hollywood. It's the kind of family we all wanted growing up—the kind of perfect world we always imagined. But behind the scenes June was probably a lonely, depressed housewife; Ward wasn't getting any sex; and Wally was, no doubt, pummeling his little brother Beaver.

The bad news is this: The world we live in is far from perfect. So, what are we to do? Well, we can nonchalantly follow in our parents' footsteps (and do exactly as they have done to us as a matter of habit), reacting to our environment as it predictably expects us to, or we can make a conscious choice to effect positive change in our own lives and in our children's lives. In so doing, we can heal our childhood wounds and alter our futures.

Most of the time we have the power to change our lives. But unfortunately, many of us choose to remain trapped in a cocoon. After all, freeing ourselves takes effort. Instead we sit and wait, hoping change will find us. Jehovah's Witnesses are masters of this. Their idealistic future, i.e., living on a paradise Earth, is the magnetic "draw" that pulls so many people into the cult. Who wouldn't want to live this way—free from all disease and crime? But there is one major flaw in the JW belief system. The dream manufactured by the Jehovah's Witnesses is just that—a dream.

Instead of hoping for divine intervention to take care of everything for us, I believe it is up to all of us to create a little heaven on this planet in the time we are living here. This is our reality. This is our life. This is our choice.

Granted, if we do nothing, eventually change will find us (remember, the only constant in life is change), but waiting might involve years of needless suffering. If you are tired of living an unfulfilling life and want marvelous things to occur on your timetable, *you* must be the agent for change. Change is the catalyst for personal growth, and growth promotes happiness.

We must understand, however, that happiness isn't produced externally. Many people aren't happy simply because they are waiting for some outside force to tap them on the head with a happiness wand. Happiness isn't a present you receive when you meet someone wonderful, come into wealth, or find the perfect job. These things can make your life more enjoyable and provide security. But what happens when you lose your lover, money or job? You become unhappy. No, this isn't happiness.

To find lasting, *core* happiness you have to peel away life's layers and uncover what makes you feel whole. You have to learn to be truly comfortable in your own skin and love yourself unconditionally, even when you know your mother, your father, your spouse or your child cannot. You have to manage your life, set and achieve goals, and appreciate all you have, all you are. Instead of waiting for someone to bring you flowers, you have to till the soil and tend to your own garden. And sometimes when your life feels like it's spiraling out of control, you have to fight like Hell to hold onto the real *you*.

Parallel #2—Guardian Angels

My father encountered guardian angels, as did I. And I have no doubt that future generations will encounter them as well, if only they are intuitive enough to hear them when they speak.

Parallel #3—Abuse

My abuse at the hands of teachers and Derek's abuse by a daycare provider strikes yet another parallel.

I was reliving the experience in my life when my mother failed to protect me from that schoolteacher who paddled me. By vehemently standing up for my son when Sheba abused him, I made a conscious choice to rectify a mistake that had occurred earlier in my life. Through my modern-day battles, I triumphed over the demons from my past and saved myself, my son and perhaps many other children as well. I turned a terrible negative into a wonderful positive.[19]

Parallel #4—Isolation

The isolation I experienced both as a teen and as a young adult was my way of repeating history. Because I had lived *all alone in the world* as a Jehovah's Witness for nine years, that lifestyle, although undesirable, became the norm in my life. I couldn't see it at the time but the familiarity, although distressing, was somewhat comforting as well. My mother had built the foundation for me to live in isolation, and I allowed Sean to erect the walls. Living inside this box, with Sean on the other side of the wall, allowed me to relive my childhood. It allowed me to try to make right the person on

---

[19] Fortunately, the incident with the "Queen" was so brief that today Derek has little memory of it, or her.

the other side of the wall (my mother/my husband). As a child, I *couldn't* yell to my mother, "Here I am. Love me! Choose me over your religion." However, after I became an adult and Sean appeared in my life, I *could* yell to Sean, "Here I am. Love me! Choose me over your addictions." Being with Sean gave me the voice I needed, the voice I never had as a child. Sometimes we just need to be heard.

I suspect few of us ever see any parallels in our lives because we try to repress the negative memories so that we can live peacefully in the present. However, we must not, indeed we *cannot*, shut out our past. It is part of who we are. If we can discover the parallels in our lives, perhaps we can help future generations—our children and their children— learn to love and accept themselves in this marvelous, but sometimes cruel, world. If only we could step back, dig deeper, and see past the daily job routine, the runny noses, the bills, the chores and the endless day-to-day struggles. Maybe then we might all find some meaning in our suffering.

Granted, the past is over. We certainly can't go back in time and change things, but we can start now to make a brand new ending. The past, present and future are indelibly intertwined—more than we'd like to admit. *Our past*, our future's past, *is being written today*. What are you writing on yours?

As you take your own personal journey through life, I **hope** you too will gain remarkable insight. Perhaps your life will open up into a world that is more colorful than those effervescent wings you've grown. Please don't be afraid to become a butterfly and take flight. If I could do it, so can *you*. Indeed, so can you!

THE END

Afterword

My life, riddled with early-on "learning opportunities" (not failures) followed by tangible success—living my life in my own way—is a testament to the power of self-love and acceptance. And what would I do if I had it to do all over?

I wouldn't change a thing.

It's made me who I am and has given me the resolve that I can handle anything that comes my way. I'm no longer afraid. I've learned that I alone decide whether I should feel happy and loved or depressed and "all alone in the world."

I still carry my childhood with me in my heart. I always will. Although pieces of my childhood have fallen away into the JW abyss, some pieces remain. After I moved away from Pennsylvania, for years I couldn't recall anything positive because so much negativity and fear had dominated my childhood. I had blocked out the pottery from the stream, the umbrella plants, the hayloft, my bike with the banana seat and white wicker basket—the things that brought joy into my life. Slowly, as I began to heal, those memories started to come back to me. And, oh, how I cherish them!

My still-cocooned mother, siblings, nephews, and niece haven't been a part of my life since the day I left the cult over twenty-five years ago. I respect their right to believe what they want even though they refuse to accept mine. Still, should any religion have the right to scoop out an individual's identity and dismantle their family unit? Is that what the Divine Being had in mind? Weren't we instilled with independent thought for a reason?

Most Jehovah's Witnesses who read my memoir will scoff at what I've done with my life. They will say I have condemned my son to death. They will insist he is living in a "broken home," a term used to refer to "disadvantaged" children being raised in single-parent households. Alas, how wrong they are on both accounts! Despite all the tragedy and hardship Derek and I have encountered, our lives are blessed. Derek could have been raised in a broken home, had his mother chosen to remain in dysfunction as either a Jehovah's Witness or as the wife of an alcoholic. No, our home, our family, isn't broken. Quite to the contrary, it has been *fixed*.

As a Jehovah's Witness teenager, I learned firsthand one of life's most valuable lessons: A child's emotional state is comparable to a fragile butterfly. If we hold them too tightly, we will crush them and disable their flight. But if we throw them into the wind before they are ready to fly, they will fall to the ground and possibly be trampled. As parents, we need to continually monitor our grip.

Elizabeth Stone once wrote:

> Making the decision to have a child is momentous. It is to decide forever to have your heart go walking around outside your body.

No one knows this better than any parent who has held back the tears as they've said good-bye to their preschooler the first day of daycare, their five-year-old on the first day of kindergarten, or their eighteen-year-old as they go off to college. Losing that physical closeness seems unnatural, even though our heart goes with them. That's why we sometimes hold on too tightly. We must always remember, though, that while mothers and fathers need their children and children need their mothers and fathers, we all need our independence too. Balance is the key.

My **hope** and **dream** today is that my son will grow up with enough insight to be the father to his children that his father never was to him, just as I grew up to be the mother to him that my mother never was to me.

When Derek flies away from me someday, I know he will come back, because I will have helped him emerge from his protective childhood cocoon and will have supported and cheered him during his first flight. I will have given him both roots and wings. It takes unconditional, selfless love to be an effective parent, to provide support and then set our child free to fly like a butterfly. It's never easy to let go, but it's what we were designed as parents to do. It's what we *must* do.

Perhaps by telling my story, my grandchildren and great-grandchildren will know me long after I am gone. Perhaps they will be raised with boundless, unconditional love, passing my legacy, my **hopes** and **dreams**, to future generations. And lastly, perhaps my story will provide comfort to those who have lost a family member in some way. If I accomplish any of these things, all of the many hours I have spent in front of the computer, editing and rewriting, opening up my life and bleeding my soul will have been worth it.

The Truth is, no matter what has happened in the past or what will happen in the future, Derek and I are family. **We will always be a family.** My love for Derek is not conditional. And *nothing* and *no one* on this Earth will ever change that—not even a nice Jehovah's Witness knocking on our door.

Appendix
Puzzling Through Poetry

I wrote the following for my friend, Jennifer, when I was in eighth grade. She compassionately helped me get through a three-hour therapy session with our school's guidance counselor:

<u>My Friend</u>

In all the years I've known you
You've never let me down
When life seemed dull or painful
You turned my world around

Sometimes I felt like giving up
But you somehow made me strong
By being concerned and showing love
When my feelings seemed all wrong

You've stuck by me through thin and thick
And I know we'll always be close
Because of all the friends I have today
You're the one I treasure most

My aunt was the "something in your environment" (in the last verse) that helped change the course of my life.

Changes

Things seem so difficult at times
There are many arguments about ideas and belief
Nothing in life fits together—nothing seems to rhyme
There seems to be no sign of relief.

You don't want to hurt those you care about
So it must be broken gently
You must prove you can be on your own—leave no doubt
That I am not you—I am *me*!

Then, just as you think your world is falling in
Something in your environment seems to change life
Then suddenly, instead of losing, you begin to win
Soon gone are many tensions, frustrations, and strife.

When I was about fifteen I wrote "Childhood Memories and Growing Up Pains" in a mere forty minutes. My most vivid memory is wiping my tears away as they fell onto the notebook paper. I think this poem, more than any other, highlights my desperation and resolve to eventually change my world and leave my childhood behind.

Childhood Memories and Growing Up Pains

Parents say time and again
How they wish to be young again
To live a carefree worriless life
To be free of the troubles of everyday strife.

Childhood they say is the easiest time
But I wouldn't pay it two cents to a dime
You always must do as others say
And never do anything your own way.

Everything is so hard when you're a teen
The following is a list of what I mean:
Too old to be a child, too young to be an adult
And tell me is that our fault?

I could write forever about the pain
Friendships broken and going insane
And boyfriends who say they love you
But break your heart by not being true.

Searching for identity is the hardest I'd say
No one knows who they are anyway
Choosing a right road is not hard to do
If you follow instincts and just be you.

Childhood Memories and Growing Up Pains
(continued)

Now I have to ask those who wanted to be young
Aren't you glad your childhood's done?
When you said that, were you sober?
As far as I'm concerned, I'd never do it over.

I'd rather leave it far in the past
Oh, how long it seemed to last
So before you adults say that once more
Think of the miserable/confusing life you had before!

When I was in my senior year of school, I felt utter frustration towards my family, especially my mother. It would take many years before she would learn how much her religious beliefs tormented me.

Frustration, Confusion, Disillusion

Frustration, confusion, disillusion
Are not simply fragments of my mind
In reality they occupy my soul
While my freedom the fanatic seeks to bind.

Frustration, confusion, disillusion
No longer obscure my aim of sight
I discern my goal by exceeding oppression
With boldness I must shrewdly and secretly fight.

Frustration, confusion, disillusion
With a decade of constant painful mass
Will cease to control my developing world
With brief duration she and they will swiftly pass!

Good-Bye

You think that I am happy
'Cause you see my smiling face
But if you just look closer
You will see a basket case.

Your pressures and restrictions
Have boiled to the point
That I can't move or think
They have spread through every joint.

You say you want the best for me
But how will I learn and grow
If following instructions
Is the only thing I know?

Can't you see this is my life
And that you've ripped it apart
By living it as your very own
Right from the very start.

Don't force ideas upon me
Please, Ma, let me form my own
For what you reap from life
Is only what you've sown.

Please see that I'm a person
Not just a dumb rag doll
That you control with words
That follows your every call.

I know you'll never understand
That I just want to be me
Please don't cry when I say good-bye
I'm leaving—I must be free.

Love. What a perplexing emotion it is—whether you are twelve or forty. After I saw my first crush doting after another girl, these words gushed from my heart like a flash flood. Unfortunately, I'm not sure I understand the opposite sex any better today.

Lost Love

When we first met one summer day
While playing volleyball
You laughed and teased and seemed so free
Which wasn't true at all.

The night fell soon and I went home
You said that you would write
The letter came within two days
And love, you stole my sight.

You seemed depressed and quite confused
You did not know just why
When to yourself be critical
Your words I would defy.

Weeks passed so quickly by it seemed
And I did not see you
Time did not make your heart grow fond
Your letters were not new.

One day at least we soon did meet
And oh, how you did stare
I hoped that things had changed for good
I thought that you did care.

Lost Love
(continued)

I made you happy when depressed
Now I have got the blues
You did not feel the things for me
That I had felt for you.

And as you spoke I saw the light
That you were not my guy
You clung to me just like a leech
Then slowly said good-bye.

I found peace when I stopped fighting the inevitable (the JW rules), enjoyed the solitude of a summer day, absorbed the sun on my face and reminded myself that my enslavement was nearing an end. An eighteen-year-old woman with so many hopes and dreams ahead of her penned the sheer joy contained in the following two poems:

Spring Is...

A time we appreciate everything around
Every breath we breathe, detail, aroma and sound
When winter's bitter cold blanket is at last gone
We wake to a bright sun-filled, joyous new dawn.

The birds chirp their melodies of songs through the day
While many carefree children outside are at play
I sit here in peace just watching the world go by
Under the colorful sunset of a gray-blue sky.

The sweet smell of fresh-cut grass makes me come alive
To the wonder of spring, for happiness to strive
We never become bored of this flower season
To live for its beauty is good enough reason.

The Best Things in Life Are Free

In this hectic world where no one slows down
Have we stopped to see or to hear a sound?
When money seems to make all men survive
Do not the free things make man alive?

To feel a cool breeze on a summer day
To hear the laughter of children at play
To drink chilling water from a babbling brook
Are all experiences contained in no book.

To see a puppy bounce awkwardly around
To hear a lost child cry when she is found
To behold a bright rainbow after a storm
Helps me appreciate life in every form.

To reach out and hold someone that you love
To pick a spring daisy, so soft like a dove
To have fun with friends when there's nothing to do
Be silent and notice the beauty 'round you.

Prior to leaving Pennsylvania, I mailed my first lover, Alex, a permanent reminder of my adoration. (Al and Sam are his brothers.)

I Will Never Forget

I will never forget your big blue eyes
And how they gazed in mine
They held a mystery that sparkled bright
Like stars they seemed to shine.

I will never forget your gorgeous smile
Because it was unique
It made me feel special and warm inside
But made my knees grow weak.

I will never forget your sweet, soft lips
For from them words did flow
Words that were gentle, never harsh or cruel
Their meaning I couldn't know.

I will never forget, oh no I won't
"That's just the way I am"
I love you Alex and will think of you
As well as Al and Sam.

As a young adult, I really struggled to find my place in the world while I fought to gain my family's acceptance. In an effort to relieve a bit of the sadness that was brewing inside, I was inspired to write the following:

<u>Life Isn't What It Used To Be</u>

Life seems funny to me sometimes
As a young child I was happy and carefree
I remember my small allowance of just a dime
And the mud pies I used to create from the stream.

I used to play dolls for hours and hours
Never tiring of the same old toys I had
In springtime I'd pick dozens of flowers
Presenting them to my mom to see her smile.

My cousins and I would jump into the hay
Never afraid to climb the barn loft, high above
We would ride our bikes the entire day
Pretending the telephone poles were green lights.

I used to do all these things you see
Until the age of ten, then it was forbidden
I stopped laughing and became someone else
I started crying 'cause I didn't understand why.

For years I grew up alone and afraid
Wondering if I'd survive that way
My parents didn't know me—the person they'd made
Because communication lines were closed.

Life Isn't What It Used To Be
(continued)

So many times I did try to talk
But they wouldn't accept how I felt at all
Back then it seemed they had hearts of pure rock
Because they were always right, and I was wrong.

So I clung to my friends and those who did care
Holding my frustration and sorrow inside
Small was the social life and smile I did bear
But huge were the hopes and dreams I concealed.

I looked to a time when I could be me
And learn about the world I was protected from
I wanted to travel far away to see
If I could be happy and fulfill my dream.

It seems like yesterday and it's still in my mind
Yet I have to forget and go on living
Because there's so much in life still to find
To learn about and at last discover.

My parents write that they wish I were there
But they still don't know me, or know why I'm here
I've found happiness, a home, and people who care
To go back to what was would only destroy me.

Life isn't what it used to be, I know
But I'm not still that same little girl
And life isn't as funny as it used to be
Because the two people I love just won't let go.

I recognized my own vulnerability in the following poem, written about Sean, after meeting him in Colorado when I was eighteen:

<u>How Am I Supposed to React?</u>

Just what is love supposed to be
I do not really know
I've pondered this question endlessly
Is it my friend or foe?

Living in a world all alone
Made me self-reliant
Liberal and strong, willing to condone
And just a bit defiant.

I've never met anyone who's cared
About me – for who I am
Therefore I feel uptight and scared
To know a guy like Sean.

Many emotions run wild inside
But I must always be strong
I mustn't ever show how much I've cried
For dwelling on the past is wrong.

So I'll live each day as it comes
Enjoying my life with this man
I'll try to revive what once was numb
And learn whatever I can.

I shared some brutally raw emotion with my dad during our "Come to Jesus Meeting":

Guilt Trips

You ask me how I could leave
Even though it's been explained
A million times the anger I felt
And especially the pain.

You call and talk of dying
And how everyone is gone
There's nothing left in life
For which you can go on.

Stop trying to pull me down
To the unhappiness you feel
Most parents do want happy kids
And mine is finally real.

I can't make you happy
Only you can make your life
For happiness comes from within
And *you* must fight the strife.

Stop trying to explain Ma's actions
I know them all too well
There's no excuse for what she's done
And she can go to Hell.

I was smart to move to Colorado
In PA I'd live close by
To a "family" who won't speak to me
Not even to just say "Hi."

To My Estranged Mother

Your face is a memory
Your voice like a dream
Surrounded by clouds
Forever unseen.

You know I'm alive
But I'm like a stranger
Someone you'd encounter
But avoid, fearing danger.

You've chosen a life
Of which I can't be a part
You condemn me so freely
With your silent, cruel heart.

You're missing so much
But you just cannot see
How your man-made faith
Destroys you and me.

I can only hope
As you come to the end
You'll realize the loss
Of what could have been.

While Derek was being severely neglected at SUX, I released my angst through poetry after I arrived one morning to work in tears. This poem is framed and still hangs on his bedroom wall today, with a small piece of his original baby blanket tucked inside.

To My Precious Baby, Derek
You are my life, my existence begun
The reason I live, my little one
You need me, it's true and cry when I go
But the anguish of leaving, I try not to show.

I think about you and feel so incomplete
Tears come easily and I suffer defeat
It is so unnatural that we must part
For you are a part of me, my soul, my heart.

And though I know I can't always be there
To be away from you now seems so unfair
For time slips by quickly; seems you were just born
But now my memory is old and worn.

Oh, what I would do to be able to hold you more
To protect you, love you, and make you secure.

And though at times I'd like to be left alone,
To taste independence which is often unknown
I soon miss your sweet smile and big blue eyes
And the way you look at me as though I'm so wise.

I wish I could take your fears and toss them away
And protect you from all that does hurt you each day
I wish you could understand all that's been said
So I could dry your tears and help you see
That you are my life, my existence begun
I'll always love you, my precious son.

Recommended Reading

Reinventing Yourself by Steve Chandler: This is a superb book for those coming out of any dysfunctional environment. Steve shows you how to go from victim to owner and reestablish your misplaced power and confidence.

Truth or Consequences by Roy Milton: This is a heart-breaking love story about a former Jehovah's Witness Elder who lost his childhood sweetheart and daughter to the Watchtower Bible and Tract Society.

Awakening of a Jehovah's Witness by Diane Wilson: If you want to understand not only the emotional aspect of being a Jehovah's Witness but also the organization's theology, doctrinal flip-flops and failed prophesies, invest some time in this comprehensive book.

Visions of Glory: A History and a Memory of Jehovah's Witnesses by Barbara Grizzuti Harrison: Discover how the Watchtower organization was started by one man and go inside the cult's headquarters with someone who used to work at Bethel. See www.exjws.net/vg.htm .

Children Learn What They Live by Dorothy Law Nolte: A "must-have" for parents who care about rearing their children by their own example utilizing discipline, love and respect. Every new parent should own this book.

Daddy, Daddy Be There by Candy Dawson Boyd and Floyd Cooper: See the world through children's eyes as they plead for fathers to "be there." This book features kids and adults from various ethnic backgrounds, giving it a universal appeal.

OUT OF THE COCOON
A Young Woman's Courageous Flight
From the Grip of a Religious Cult

By

Brenda Lee

To purchase *autographed* cop(ies) of this book, send this order form (please print legibly) along with payment (indicated below), **payable to Love & Light Literary, LLC**, c/o

"Out of the Cocoon"
P.O. Box 16668
Golden, CO 80402 USA

PRICE:

• Inside U.S.: $19.95 each, personal check or money order (includes shipping/handling)
• Outside U.S.: $27.95 USD each, money orders *only* (includes shipping/handling)

SHIP BOOK(s) TO:

First/Last Name: _____

Address: _____

City: _____

State: _____

Zip Code: _____ Country: _____

Purchaser's E-mail address (if there are questions): _____

Autograph this book for (name): _____

Note to Customer: Please feel free to copy this order form if you want to purchase books for more than one person/address. Please rest assured that your personal information will remain confidential. Delivery Time: Within the U.S., please allow up to 4 weeks. Outside the U.S., please allow up to 6 weeks.